# A WORLD OF WOMEN

# IRENE DANCYGER

# A
# World of Women

## An illustrated history of women's magazines

### Gill and Macmillan

First published 1978 by
Gill and Macmillan Ltd
15/17 Eden Quay
Dublin 1
with associated companies in
London, New York, Delhi, Hong Kong,
Johannesburg, Lagos, Melbourne,
Singapore, Tokyo

7171 0730 2

Filmsetting by Keyspools Ltd, Golborne, Lancs.
Printed in Great Britain by Fletcher & Sons Ltd, Norwich

# Contents

*To 'Bridge', Jane and Paul,*
*with love and gratitude*

# *Preface*

ACKNOWLEDGMENTS and thanks are due to Lady Georgina Coleridge, Miss Katherine Fryer, Miss Dorothea Abbott, Librarian of Birmingham Polytechnic College of Art Library, Miss Jocelyn Morris, former Curator of Warwick Museum, the staff of Warwick Records Office, Mrs Margaret Slater, Leamington Spa Art Gallery, the staffs of the British Library Reading Room, Bloomsbury, the British Museum Newspaper Library, Colindale and Leamington Spa Library, to Mr Geoffrey T. Large, Librarian of the National Magazine Company, Chestergate House, London, the late Mr Peter Lawrence, former editor of *Woman*, Miss Beatrix Miller, editor of *Vogue*, Miss Joan Grahame, editor of *The Lady*, Miss Psyche Pirie, editor *Homes & Gardens*, Mr Jack Hampshire, Baby Carriage Collection Museum, Biddenden, Kent, Mr Ron Hallet, Assistant Secretary, National Union of Journalists; also to Mr Vincent Kinane, The Library, Trinity College, Dublin, and to the editors and columnists who spared me time for interviews.

Thanks are also due to the photographers, to Mr Michael Gill of Gill and Macmillan for his kindness and encouragement, to Mrs 'Beattie' Marshall for suggesting the title – and last but not least to my husband, son and daughter for their assistance and patience.

# *Foreword*

ANY history of women's magazines must be so much more than that, because it is also a history of the women who read them. Their pages act as a permanent record of changing tastes, ambitions, status and life-style.

Where else could such an authentic source of information be found? Since the first 'magazine' was published early in the eighteenth century, it has taken about two hundred years for a major magazine industry to be established in Britain, where, unlike any other country in the world, magazines are mainly bought by women. Our men, it seems, still prefer newspapers.

Irene Dancyger's most interesting book traces the origins and development of women's magazines, and shows clearly the extraordinary staying-power of the problem page and of romantic fiction. How little we have changed! Like their readers, magazines are here to stay, but more colourful, more outspoken, although still as practical as ever, as friendly and as entertaining. It has been a pleasure to be associated with this book which makes a most valuable contribution to publishing history.

Lady Georgina Coleridge.

# Introduction

WORDSWORTH, were he alive, might still lament 'what man has made of man'. *A World of Women*, a review of what for three centuries some women's magazines have tried to make of woman, may, it is hoped, produce a happier reaction.

'There is nothing, however seemingly trivial', wrote the editor of *The New Lady's Magazine* in 1791, 'which can come under the inspection of the contemplative or debout mind without affording some degree of profit.' Nothing, as Blake who saw 'a world in a grain of sand' knew, is without significance. A word, a glance, a gesture may convey more than a dozen dictionaries. So these ephemeral journals 'holding a mirror' if not up to man, then certainly up to women, may reveal truths lacking in written-from-hindsight histories.

Within the limitations of some 50,000 words no account could be comprehensive. Volumes could be written on any of the subjects covered. Equally informative journals had to be omitted, screeds of fascinating material left out. Where possible I have tried to show how far those included reflected, or surprisingly failed to reflect their day. Depressingly, throughout the centuries one conclusion recurs, that if Justice is blindfolded it is to ensure her ignorance of how heavily the scales are weighted against our sex. It could scarcely have been otherwise. Woman, enslaved by her biology, was dependent upon man. He who pays the piper calls the tune, and since time began his tune has conditioned her to dance to his will, accept second-rate citizenship, the belief that her 'true function in life was to minister to his needs and comforts'. The resultant tragic waste of talent throughout generations of women was summarised by Sidney Smith. 'The finest faculties in the world are confined to trifles utterly unworthy of their richness and strength.'

That some of that 'richness and strength' was channelled into causes weightier than Berlin wool samplers, pin cushions and pudding recipes was due in no small part to women's magazines. Often divided on their views of female franchise, they were at one in their fight against social injustice. Their campaigns against slums, labour exploitation, homelessness, unemployment, prison conditions, workhouses and the treatment of inmates of 'lunatic asylums'; their fight for better terms of employment, for widening opportunities for women, were unflagging and impressive.

In the less contentious spheres of home-making, child-care, cooking, handicrafts, fashion, decor, housewifery, and beauty their influence has been immeasurable.

Today (in the Western world at least) thanks to medical, scientific and educational advances, woman as previously 'cast'—the prematurely aged, involuntarily pregnant, overworked drudge, or pampered, helpless, pin-headed doll—need exist no longer. Released by contraceptives from her biological helplessness, woman may for the first time in history make her own choices, stand on her own feet. She may decide whether or not to have a family, and upon its size. No longer at the mercy of the disabling monthly period, she may also soon be freed from the menopause. No longer 'on the shelf' at thirty, 'old' at forty or fifty, 'senile' at sixty or seventy, she may pursue a variety of roles, live untrammelled by the taboos and shibboleths that shackled her ancestresses.

As her interests increase, so too does the scope for a widening, exciting and challenging women's magazine content. The remark once made by former editor of *Woman*, Mary Grieve, that she 'would no more expect to see an article on finance in a women's magazine, than one on weaning in the Financial Times' no longer applies. From cosmetics to carburettors, bead-work to bricklaying, politics to paper panties, there are no longer subjects 'unsuitable for women'. Freed from the metaphorical whalebone stays of 'women's interests', today's editors may extract what pearls they will from a veritable world of oysters.

Like their predecessors, today's journals seek to entertain, to inform, to reassure. Like their predecessors, today's readers are, to quote IPC Director Patricia Lamburn, 'looking for a friend'. And as always—'it is upon the personality of the editor that the personality of that friend will almost entirely depend'.

It is to these friends, and to all who contribute to the publication and production of these 'brief and abstract chronicles of the times' that I express thanks, and wish ever-increasing and on-going success.

Irene Dancyger.

# CHAPTER ONE

# *Portents*

I F as may be reasonably argued, 'the proper study of mankind' likewise embraces woman, a proposition to which neither side is likely to object, it may be instructive to glance at the reading matter which for the past two hundred years or more has fashioned woman's thinking.

As early as 1487, coming events cast their shadows before, when one Jacques Legrand published his *Booke of Good Manners*, a treatise on etiquette, later followed by *The Booke of Carving and Sewing, Cookerie and Carving, A Booke of Strange Inventions called the First Part of Needlework*, and *A Schoolhouse for the Needle*.

In today's jargon it was an expanding market. Already in Henry VIII's reign, court ladies enjoyed an education similar to their brothers', and John Knox's 'monstrous regimen of women', Elizabeth I, Mary Stuart of Scotland and Catherine de' Medici of France, set a pattern for women's learning and liberation later lost sight of until our own time.

Priests, prelates, pundits, preachers raged against women's 'love of folly', dancing, cosmetics, fashions; scribbled furious edicts dictating how women should conduct themselves in every conceivable contingency in life, in a manner most conducive to the comfort, contentment and convenience of that most remarkable of all creations, Man.

For the first time in the eternal war of the sexes, women could retaliate in print. A ding-dong battle kept the presses turning with publications such as: *Jane Anger, her Protection of Women. To defend them against the scandalous reportes of a late Surfeiting lover, and other venerians that complain to be overcloyed with women's kindnesses*, London 1589; *The worming of a madde dogge, or a soppe for Cerberus, the Jailor of Hell*, by Constantia Munday, London 1617; *Ester hath hanged Haman, or an Answere to a Lewd pamphlet entitled 'The arrainment of Woman', with the arrainment of Lewd, Idle, Froward and Inconstant men and Husbands*, by Ester Sowerman, London 1617; *Tattle-well Mary and hit-him-home Joan, the woman's sharpe revenge, or an answer to Sir Seldom Sober . . . in defence of women*, London 1640.

Echoes of their arguments against the injustices suffered by women at the hands of men, reverberate down the ages. Equally familiar are the questions that preoccupied Lucca Tomaso Buoni's *Problems of Beautie and all human affections*, translated into English during the reign of Queen Elizabeth—who, indeed, may have read it herself. Like today's Advice columns, the contents were arranged in the form of questions and answers:

Herbs were
essential for
Elizabethan
cooking,
medicine and
beauty recipes.
*Gerarde's
Herbal*, 1633.

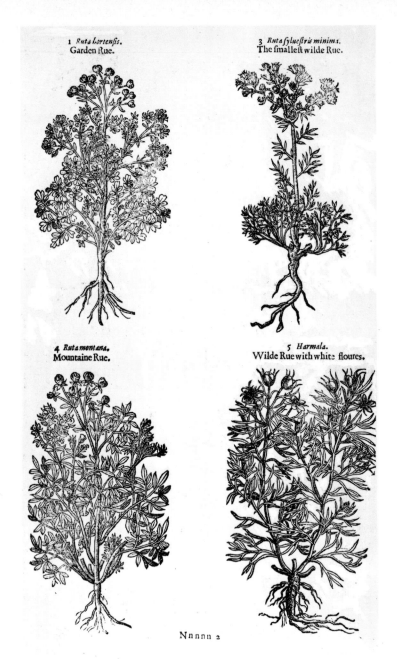

1 *Ruta Lortensis.*
Garden Rue.

3 *Ruta sylvestris minims.*
The smallest wilde Rue.

4 *Ruta montana.*
Mountaine Rue.

5 *Harmala.*
Wilde Rue with white floures.

Nnnnn 2

Q. Why is beautie enjoyed, the less esteemed?

A. Because the agent, possessing his end, in it is rested contented and satisfied; and the love enjoying that beauty which he loveth, queles his affection by the fruition of that he desired.

Q. Why doe young men prefer beautie of the body to beautie of the mind?

A. Because young men in everything show themselves credulous, whereby they turn their thoughts to everything appearing beautiful that presenteth itself to the eye, neither caring nor dreaming of any greater.

An early
specialist in
the problems
later so dear to
women's
magazines.

# PROBLEMES
## OF
## BEAVTIE

and

*all humane affections.*

## Written in Italian

by *Tho: Buoni,* cittizen
*of* Lucca.

*With a discourse of Beauty, by
the same Author.*

Tranflated into Englifh, by
*S. L.* Gent.

AT LONDON
Printed by *G. Eld,* for *Edward
Blount,* and *William Aspley.*

Q. Why doe women which are not born fayre attempt with artificial beautie to seem fayre?

A. Perhaps because there is not any woman (except they be rare) which desireth not to please some eye, and therefore being well assured they cannot please any without special beautie, wherein they sometimes proceed so far that they onely exceede their ability, but work themselves into a contrary affect.

5

Q. Why do not lovers, in the presence of those they love, know not how to frame their speech?

A. The once vehement intention of the mind overtakes the tonge . . . he has little use for any other of his senses, therefore it is no marvel if man stands mute in the presence of their loves when they should speak, or he uttereth his mind stammeringly . . . tremblingly, and grow pale . . . and utter their conceits many times brokenly.

Q. Why is the hatred of women without end or measure?

A. Perhaps, because loving man with a strong and earnest affection . . . and afterwards discerning a false heart, or a mind unthankful, they presently turn their love to hate.

Other observations remain undimmed by time.

'There is no greater felicity in the whole Empire of Love than the certain assurance of the true heart of his best beloved.'

'Far distance . . . [from the loved one] doth engender that griefe in the heart that can hardly be expressed to themselves, much less to those not acquainted with like miseries . . .'

Faced with 'lovesickeness' you could turn to 'recipes to comforte the hearte and take away melancholy.'

'Take of the joice of Borage, four pounds, the flowers of the Borage, halfe a pounde. Let these stand infused in hote embers fourteene hours, then being strained and clarified, put two of good sugar [two pounds] and boile it to a sirrop.'

Or, as 'An electuary for the Passion of the Hearte' advised: 'Take damask roses half-blowne, out of their whites and stamp them very fine, and strayn out the juyce very strong; moisten it in the stamping with a little damask rose-water, then put thereof fine powder sugar and boyle it gently to a thin syrup; then take the powders of amber, pearls and rubies of each half a dram, amber-grease one scruple, and mingle them with the said syrup till it be somewhat thicke, and take a little thereof on a knife's point, morning and evening.'

Protest as men might against 'box complexions', 'abominable oyles and daubings', 'shamefaced payntings', women 'anxious to appear pleasing in the eyes of at least one man' resorted to cosmetics.

Queen Elizabeth's pale skin and auburn hair set the fashion. Red and white complexions, topless gowns were 'in'. Tragically the ceruse lead compound that produced the desired lily-white face and breasts brought other, often fatal side-effects:

> In a yere or lesses
> Or two at most, my lovely, lively bride
> Is turned a hagge, a fury by my side,
> With hollow, yellow teeth, or none perhaps,
> With stinking breath, swart cheeks and hanging chaps.
> With wrinkled necke, and stouping as she goes,
> With druling mouth, and with a snivelling nose.

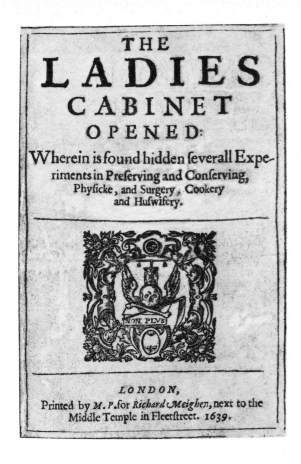

THE
LADIES
CABINET
OPENED:
Wherein is found hidden severall Experiments in Preserving and Conserving, Physicke, and Surgery, Cookery and Huswifery.

*NON PLVS*

LONDON,
Printed by *M. P.* for *Richard Meighen*, next to the Middle Temple in Fleetstreet. 1639.

THE
QUEENS CLOSET
OPENED.
Incomparable Secrets in *Physick*, *Chirurgery*, *Preserving*, *Candying*, and *Cookery*;

As they were presented to the
QUEEN

By the most Experienced Persons of our Times, many whereof were honoured with her own practice, when she pleased to descend to these more private Recreations.

*Never before published.*

Transcribed from the true Copies of her MAJESTIES own Receipt Books, by *W. M.* one of her late servants.

*Vivit post funera Virtus.*

Printed for *Nathaniel Brook* at the *Angel* in *Cornhill*, 1655.

Safer, perhaps, to use alternative beauty aids.

'Haire as yellow as golde' could be simulated with 'the rine of rhubarb steeped in white wine, and after you have washed your heade with it, you shall wet your haires with a spunge, and let them lay by the fire or in the sunne'.

Not all gentlemen, as Shakespeare's Sonnets to a Dark Lady prove, preferred blondes: 'To make haire grow black, take a little acqua fortis, put therein a groat or sixpence, as to the quantity of the aforesaid water, then let them both dissolve before the fire, then dip a small spunge in the said water, and wet your hair or beard therewith, but touch not the skin.' Which suggests that not only women employed beauty aids.

'Helpe was at hande' also for bearded ladies. 'Take the shell of fifty-two egges, beat them small, and still them with a good fire, and with the water annoynt yourself where you would have the haire off. Or cats dung that is hard and dryed, beate to a powder and temper with strong vinegar and annoynted on the place, will serve.'

Elizabethan women not only dyed their hair. They sometimes cropped it, and wore men's clothing. A contemporary writer, condemning alike 'the foppish,

Left.
Frontispiece of
*The Ladies Cabinet Opened*, 1639.

Right.
Frontispiece of
*The Queens Closet Opened*, 1655. The queen referred to was Queen Henrietta Maria, wife of Charles I.

7

Left and Right. Avoiding plague and pestilence was literally a matter of life and death for the Elizabethan family. *The Treasurie or Closet of Hidden Secrets*, 1600, advised its readers 'to keep your houses, yards, backsides, streets and channels clean' from the dangers of 'standing puddles, dunghills and corrupt moistures which engender stinking and filthy vapours'; 'to suffer no dogs nor cats to come unto your houses'; and 'to air your rooms . . . with charcoal fires'.

THE
Treasurie of hidden
*Secrets.*

Commonlie called,
The Good-huſwiues Cloſet of prouiſion,
*for the health of her Housbold.*

Gathered out of ſundry experiments, lately practiſed by men
of great knowledge : And now newly enlarged, with diuers neceſſary
Phiſicke helpes, and knowledge of the names and naturall diſpo-
ſition of diſeaſes, that moſt commonly happen
to men and vvomen.

Not impertinent for euery good Huſwife to vſe in her
houſe, amongſt her owne familie.

AT LONDON,
Printed by *I. R.* for Edward White, and are to be ſold
at his ſhop at the little North doore of Paules, at the
ſigne of the Gunne. 1 6 0 0.

womanish man, and the man-woman', refers to the latter's 'shorne, powdered, borrowed haire, a naked lascivious, bawdy bosom . . . a dagger, a Highway Pistoll, and behaviour suitable of exceeding every deformitie'.

Unlike her Victorian descendant who, buttressed by cheap labour, could devote

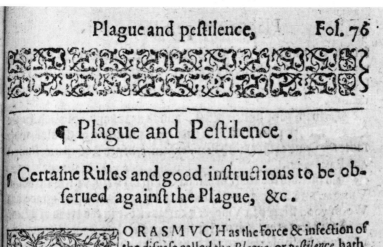

## ¶ Plague and Peſtilence .

¶ Certaine Rules and good inſtructions to be obſerued againſt the Plague, &c.

FORASMVCH as the force & infection of the diſeaſe called the *Plague* or *peſtilence*, hath heretofore bin too well knowne and felt in diuers & ſundry places of this Realme, and for that diuers Cities, Townes, & other places of this Realme, haue binne ſo grieuouſly vexed therewith: therefore (according to my ſimple ſkill and knowledge therein) I haue thought good to publiſh and make knowne vnto all, ſwell ſuch preſeruatiues as are good to be vſed, obſerued & kept by al ſorts of people for the auoyding of the ſame diſeaſe, being greatly infectious, and eaſily taken diuers and ſundry waies: as alſo for the better preſeruation of thoſe that are in health, from the infection of the diſeaſe, and to cure and order thoſe that are any way infected or grieued with the ſame: and therefore theſe things following, ought chiefely to be regarded, and fully obſerued. (Viz)

1 To keep your Houſes, Yards, Backſides, Streets, & Chennells, cleane frō al ſtanding puddles, dunghils, & corrupt moiſtures which ingender ſtinking & filthy ſauours that be noiſome, or bred infection.

2 To ſuffer no Dogs nor Cats to come into your houſes, nor to keep any your ſelues (except you dwel in ſome open place of Ayre) for that they be very dangerous, & moſt apt (of any kinde of thing) to take infection of ſicknes, & to bring it home to their Maiſters houſe: by reaſon ye they run frō place to place, & from one houſe to an other, continually feeding vpon ye vncleaneſt things that are caſt forth into ye ſtreets.

3 To ayre your rowmes (ſeuerally) with Char-cole fires, made in ſtone pans, or Chafing-diſhes, and not in Chimneys: but as you can

herself to a round of trivia, the Elizabethan woman, not dissimilar to today's career-girl-cum-housewife-cum-mother, assumed additional burdens with marriage. She had to organise and run a large staff for an almost self-sufficient household. Her family's health, food, clothing, education could depend upon her skills. Besides the

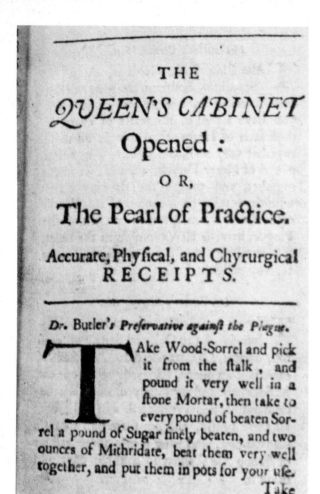

Left, Right and Opposite *The Queen's Cabinet Opened*, 1639. These pages all refer to the 'rare receipts' that this publication specialised in. (By courtesy of Leamington Spa Public Library.)

usual arts of coping with infants, cooking, and housework she had to be proficient in farming, spinning, weaving, dressmaking, pickling and conserving; to ride, sing, embroider, entertain and keep up with the Joneses.

'Shee must be up at the cracke of dawne to milke the cowes, make butter and cheese, doe the gardening, spin and weave ye clothe.' She is further urged, 'Let thy distaffe be always redye that ye be not ydlle.' Not for her the genteel 'declines', delicate swoons on the sofa. 'She must helpe her husbande fille the mucke wayne or dunge carte, dryve ye plough, lode corne, hay and suche other, and goe to market and sell butter.' Between times she must salt down meat for the winter, supervise her children's religious education and manners. Above all, she must always remain the cheerful, affectionate and attractive housewife and mother, dear to the imagination of both her contemporary tract writers, and today's admen. Not surprisingly, 'thinges' occasionally got beyond her. 'If it may fortune sometime that thou shall have so many thinges to doe thou shalt not well knowe where is best to begin, then take hede which things should be the greatest losse if it were not donne, and there begyn.'

Help, hints and advice came not from a woman's magazine but from a forerunner with the somewhat breathless title: *The Treafurie of Hidden Secrets commonlie called the Good-hufwiues Clofet of prouifion for the health of her Houfhold, Gathered out of fundry experiments lately practifed by men of great knowledge . . . of the names and naturall difpofition of difeafes that most commonly happen to men and women. Not impertinent for every good wife to ufe in her houfe amongft her owne familie.*

'Printed at London by R. for Edward White . . . to be fold at his fhop at the little North doore of Paules, at the figne of the Gunne', it addressed itself to 'Virtuous gentlewomen, Honest Matrons and Virtuous Virgins'. A lengthy foreword indicated that it offered instruction on the preparation of: 'All kinde of conserves and sirrops, sugar paste for banquetting dishes, succade, marmalade and marchpane, divers sweet distilled waters . . . fine powders for presses and chests with woollen and linnen cloathen and furres to keep them from moth-eating; and many precious oyles of sundry operations and effects. Also directions for preparations of good and wholesome kitchen physick in making good medicines, wholesome drinks and other comfortable thinges to helpe and cherish the sicke and weake in your house'.

And who could resist a recipe beginning: 'In Sommer-time when roses blow, gather them ere they be spread . . . and pluck the leaves; let them be halfe a day upon a faire board, then have a vessel with vinegar of one or two gallons; put therein a great quantitie of the saide leaves, stoppe the vessel close after they have been stirred well together.

'Let them stand a day and a night, then divide your vinegar and rose-leaves in two partes; put them in two greate glasses; set them upon a shelfe under a wall-side on the south side of your house where the sunne may come . . . the most parte of the day.

'Let them stand there the whole summer long, then strayn the vinegar and the roses, and keep the leaves, and put the new leaves of half a days gathering; the vinegar will have more odour of roses. Moreover you may make your vinegar of wine, white or redde or claret, but the redde doth most bind the bellie, and the white doth most loose.'

But life for the Elizabethan woman was not all 'gathering roses in the Sommertime', eating strawberry conserve or concocting marchpane (marzipan) 'conceits for banquetts'. Nor did the Gentlewomen, Honest Matrons or Virtuous Virgins to whom such publications, including *The Ladies Cabinet Opened* (1639), *The Queen's Closet Opened* (1665) were addressed, flinch from the mention of 'complaynts', the mere hint of which would have sent their Victorian descendants swooning in lady-like heaps. A section of the *Treasure of Hidden Secrets*, headed 'The Pearl of Practise, or phyfical and chirurgical receipts' dealt frankly with 'the swelling of the cods' 'Gonorrhea, or running of the reins, the forerunner of the foul disease'. It also contained a 'Brief treatise on urines . . . of men's urines, as well as women's; to judge by their culours which betokeneth healthe, which sickenesse, which death'. There was a 'receipt'—'to draw an arrow-head out of a wounde' and instruction for do-it-yourself surgery. 'If you feel a heaviness or oppression of spirits, a quick pulse and shortness of breath' it advised, 'open a veine for ventilation and you will find alleviation and refreshment'.

Other sections advised how to apply leeches 'for griefe of the stomacke', 'winde in the veines', 'the Falling sicknesse', how 'to holde urine', to 'cure a ricketted childe', and deal with 'the bloody flux', 'palsies, fevers, and swounding fits'; how to cure consumption with 'snails and wormes boyled in beere'. The plethora of 'receipts' against 'deathe in childe-bedde' tell their own sad tale. As do those for 'one run frantik with the Plague' or 'the Fallinge sicknesse' which, returning with 'every pretty ring-time' mocked the burgeoning May blossom, the maypole dancing, menaced 'indifferently' the babe, the chrone, the middle-aged, the 'sweet lovers' loving the springtime they might never see again.

# CHAPTER TWO

# *Beginnings* &

JOHN DUNTON, son of a country parson, and described by his contemporaries as 'a lunatick, crackbrained scribbling bookseller' (bookseller being synonymous with publisher), appears to have originated the first journal designed for women. Called *The Ladies Mercury*, it began as a monthly, then continued as a fortnightly, in 1693.

A prototype for its successors, it concerned: 'All the nice and curious questions concerning Love, Marriage, Behaviour, Dress and Humour in the Female Sex, whether Virgins, Wives or Widows'. It employed sixteen women contributors, and carried an 'Answers to Correspondents' section. Like so many innovators, Dunton died poverty-stricken, leaving others to reap the rewards of his brain-child.

Among them was John Tipper, a maths teacher from Coventry. His *Ladies Diary or Women's Almanack, or Delights for the Ingenius* was published monthly in 1711. It claimed to 'suit all conditions, Qualities and Humours', proferred advice on 'cookery, medicine, love and marriage . . . jovial and innocent amusements, education, gardening, painting and art'. Nothing was included 'that was mean or trifling . . . which would raise a Blush or Intimate an Evil Thought'.

Not unexpectedly when death in childbirth was commonplace, and an unmarried mother faced ostracism, poverty and possible starvation, editorial strictures alerted 'the Fair' against the blandishments of the wily, deceiving male.

Soon the maths master gained ascendency over the women's magazine editor. Cookery recipes and similarly feminine-orientated items were ousted in favour of maths, conundrums and brain-twisters, problems 'arithmetical, geometrical, astronomical and philosophical'. Women, he claimed to have told 'amazed foreigners'—'have as clear judgements, sprightly quick Wit and penetrating genius, and as discerning and sagacious faculties as ours'.

Diaries, Mercuries, Gazettes, Miscellanies, Intelligences, a Female Tatler, Spectator, Whisperer, Guardian, Delight, Tea-Table, Repository, Visitor, Journal, Guide and the like proliferated during the reign of Queen Anne. There were likewise the *Ladies Monthly Museum and Polite Repository of Amusement and Instruction*, the *Wives and Ladies Practical Magazine*, the *Ladies Penny Gazette*, the *Ladies World*, the *Ladies Wreath* and the *Ladies Work Table*.

News or 'intelligence' ranked almost equally with features and fiction in most of the women's journals. And with yesterday's news every bit as saleable as today's there was no lack of copy. The plague and the Great Fire of London were within living memory. Old St Paul's, built in 1240, had perished in the flames. A new man,

*The* LADIES *Diary*:
OR, THE
Woman's ALMANACK,

For the Year of our LORD, 1725.
Being the First Year after LEAP-YEAR.
Containing many Delightful and Entertaining *Particulars*,
Peculiarly Adapted for the *Use* and *Diversion* of the
FAIR-SEX.

Being the Twenty second ALMANACK ever Publish'd of that kind.

1. HAIL! happy LADIES of the *BRITISH* Isle.
On whom the GRACES and the MUSES smile,

2. LON.....d your lovely *Shape*, and matchless *Mein*,
The Wonder of our Neighb'ring Nations b..en;

3. NATURE to make your *Triumph* more compleat,
To peerless CHARMS has added piercing WIT.

NO............................-HOST,
Nor their SEMIRAMIS th' *Assyrian's* boast:
WIT joyn'd to BEAUTY, *Fame* shall now record;
Which lead more Captive than the Conqoring Sword.

Printed by *A. Wilde*, for the Company of *Stationers* 1725.

14

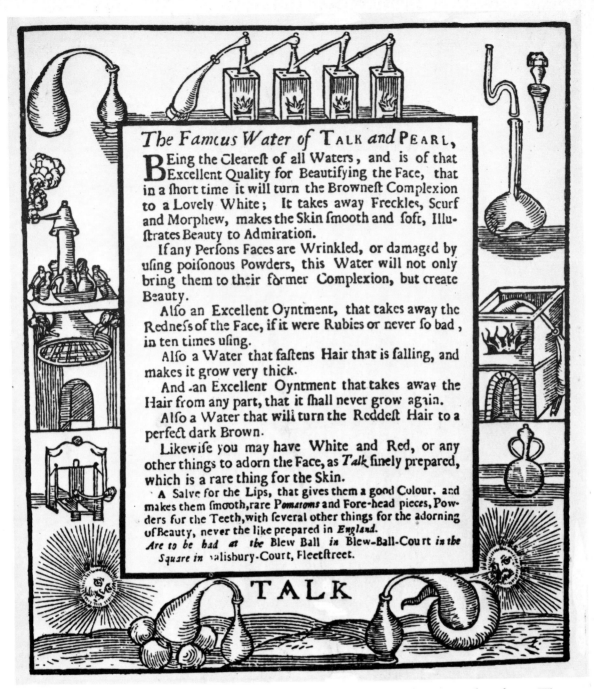

The *Famous* Water of TALK and PEARL,

BEing the Cleareſt of all Waters, and is of that Excellent Quality for Beautifying the Face, that in a ſhort time it will turn the Browneſt Complexion to a Lovely White; It takes away Freckles, Scurf and Morphew, makes the Skin ſmooth and ſoft, Illuſtrates Beauty to Admiration.

If any Perſons Faces are Wrinkled, or damaged by uſing poiſonous Powders, this Water will not only bring them to their former Complexion, but create Beauty.

Alſo an Excellent Oyntment, that takes away the Redneſs of the Face, if it were Rubies or never ſo bad, in ten times uſing.

Alſo a Water that faſtens Hair that is falling, and makes it grow very thick.

And an Excellent Oyntment that takes away the Hair from any part, that it ſhall never grow again.

Alſo a Water that will turn the Reddeſt Hair to a perfect dark Brown.

Likewiſe you may have White and Red, or any other things to adorn the Face, as *Talk* finely prepared, which is a rare thing for the Skin.

A Salve for the Lips, that gives them a good Colour, and makes them ſmooth, rare *Pomatoms* and Fore-head pieces, Powders for the Teeth, with ſeveral other things for the adorning of Beauty, never the like prepared in *England*.

*Are to be had at* the Blew Ball *in* Blew-Ball-Court *in the* Square in ſaliſbury-Court, Fleetſtreet.

TALK

Sir Christopher Wren, was designing its successor along with other new churches throughout the City. Drury Lane and Sadler's Wells theatres were well patronised. A strange flower called a Chrysanthemum had reached England via Holland and Japan. And the Dodo, such was the fashion demand for its feathers, had recently become extinct.

Ladies taking tea, introduced in 1650, could speculate about the exciting new

What copywriter could say more than this beauty ad of the 1700s?

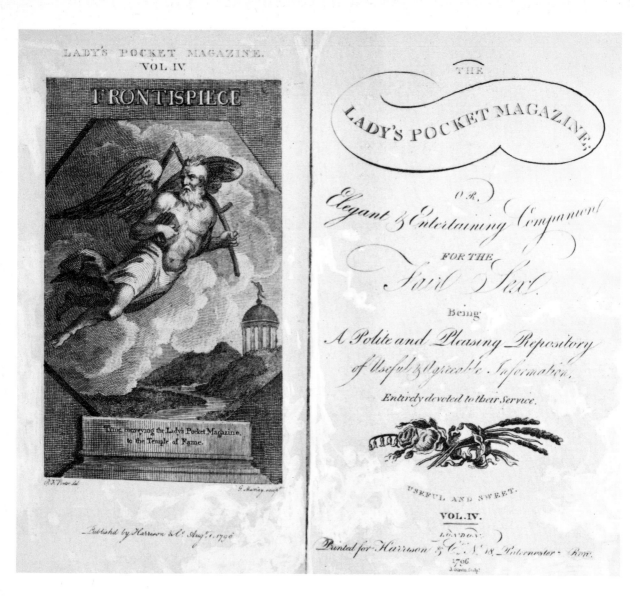

The Lady's
Pocket
Magazine,
1796;
frontispiece
and title page.

continent of Australia recently sighted by William Dampier; deplore the Massacre at Glencoe of 1692; they might also wonder about the latest wave of refugees, the Huguenots who, driven by persecution from France, were now setting up silk manufacturing in England; discuss the new fabric designs coming from far off India, a new item of furnishing known as a commode chest of drawers, or the 'best-seller' which set the vogue for 'oriental' fiction, *Oroonoko, or the History of a Royal slave* written by Mrs Aphra Behn (1640–1699), reputedly a one-time spy for Charles II.

By 1710 Beau Nash's activities in Bath, the plays at the new His Majesty's Theatre, the false-hips and eau de Cologne introduced from that city by Johann Maria Farina in 1709, provided fresh copy. By 1712 Mr Handel was composing music to delight generations to come. And an invention was patented, then forgotten, which two

16

hundred years later was to revolutionise women's lives. It was called the typewriter.

'As an alternative to the usual insipid fictions and novels and romances', one 'Ambrose Phillips', thought however to be a woman, offered 'the Fair Sex philosophical essays' in a woman's journal with the unlikely title of *The Freethinker, and Essays on Ignorance*. 'Knowledge', readers were assured, would 'in no way disfigure the features, wrinkle the skin or spoil the complexion.'

A greater 'spoiler of the complexion' and an annual killer of one-tenth of the population was the dreaded smallpox. Editing a women's magazine with another unlikely title—*The Nonsense of Commensense*—was that beauty, linguist, traveller, writer and witty antagonist of Alexander Pope, Lady Mary Wortley Montague. Her career began characteristically with her elopement with Edward, (grandson of the Earl of Sandwich), British Ambassador to Turkey. It was there, adopting the custom of the country, that she had both her children vaccinated, anticipating Jenner by some seventy-five years. An idealist, she scorned the gossip, character assassination, the innuendoes and scandal that were the lifeblood of contemporary women's journals. She wrote: 'I am unwilling to believe that there does not yet remain a great number of both sexes still capable of being delighted with what is rational. It is indeed proof of a very depraved appetite when the taste for reading must be excited by coarse raillery, or such wretched double-entendre as can only mean one Thing.'

Ironically, she herself made 'nonsense of commensense' and sizzling copy for the scandal-sheets, when at the age of fifty she absconded with her twenty-five-year-old Italian lover.

The word 'magazine' was first applied to a women's journal by bookseller Edward Cave in 1732. Encouraged by the success of his *London Magazine or Gentlemen's Monthly Intelligence*, he produced *The Ladies Magazine or Monthly Intelligence*. This included poetry, book catalogues, foreign and home news. His other (oddly titled) publications, *The Scourge*, *The Orphan*, and *The Spinster*, soon folded.

A redoubtable 'lady editoress' who, while 'considering herself far from young . . . claimed to be wise in worldly experience' was Mrs Eliza Haywood. Her *Female Spectator* catered specifically for the 'depraved appetites' despised by Lady Mary. When Mrs Haywood promised 'to lay open the secrets of Europe with a network of spies ranging from the English Spas to France, Germany and Rome', it was not political espionage she had in mind, but domestic scandal. Or, to quote Alexander Pope, 'to reveal the faults and misfortunes of both sexes, to the ruin of public fame, or disturbance of private happiness'. And there is more than a hint of sour grapes in her censures of 'The craving for admiration prevalent among young ladies . . . who run galloping in troops every evening to masquerades, balls and assemblies in Winter and in Summer, to Vauxhall, Ranalagh, Cuper's Gardens, and twenty other such places which prepare the way for . . . vicious excesses'.

A rival publication, *The Lady's Magazine*, which pledged itself to 'be free from scandalous advertisements which tend to promote vice, to encourage debauchery

Napoleon and
Josephine,
who provided
plenty of
scope for the
kind of gossip
and
speculation
dear to so
many readers
of women's
magazines –
then and now.

and unwarranted assignments', folded after the first issue. The 'advertisements'
referred to feature articles and reports. Advertisements in the modern meaning of
the word first infiltrated into women's magazines in the form of small ads, among
them one in *The Ladies Diary* of 1725 for false teeth '. . . which may be worn for years
together . . . to be taken out and put in the mouth with pleasure by persons that use
them, and are an ornament to the mouth, and greatly helpful of the speech. Also
teeth cleansed and drawn by John Watts and Samuel Ritter, who apply themselves
solely to the said business, and live in Raquet Court, Fleet Street London'.

Compared with Victorian journals whose editors regarded any hint of female
intellectuality as, if not actually immoral, then unacceptably eccentric, these
eighteenth-century publications were unusually enlightened. *The Visiter* (1724)
declared that 'brains were not necessarily incompatible with beauty'. *The Ladies
Journal* (1727) pronounced 'upon the absolute necessity for ladies to be as learned as
gentlemen'. There were even, it stated, 'undeniable instances of the Fair Sex who
have surprisingly distinguished themselves in all kinds of human literature'.

*The Ladies Magazine or the Compleat Library* (1738) not only conceded the right of the Fair Sex to have some 'vacant hours', but the necessity of their being entertained during them. Readers were told: 'Its pages contayn a very curious collection of histories, travels, novels, poems, letters etc. calculated for the benefit of persons of all ranks and conditions, but in particular with a view to the Improvement of the Fair Sex, and an amusement for their vacant hours. It may with veracity be said that a work so entertaining has never before been made Publick.'

Within its covers the eternal battle of the sexes continued. On the ever-green theme 'What is love?' it propounds: 'Love is a mixture of friendship and desire, bounded by the rules of honour and virtue. If it breaks those bounds it degenerates into lust. We know there are a great many men in the world who would make love nothing else . . . taking women in general as objects of their desires. Their seraglio is all the world . . . a bull must unavoidably be as true a lover as they.'

Not that 'the Fair' were faultless. The introduction of a *Ladies Magazine* relates: 'A young gentleman has fallen out with his mistress, and a friend endeavours to re-establish him in her good graces. The better to bring this about, he tells her that he, the lover, shall bring his pockets lined with gold, which argument they say, never failed with any woman of any age, religion or country whatsoever.'

Between-times George III sat on the throne. Britain and France squabbled in far-away Canada. And, as the *Ladies Magazine* records: 'General Wolfe died scaling the Heights of Abraham on September 13, 1759'.

'Silly girls . . . brought up to admire a Red Coat' as one reader complained, were not the only ones seized with patriotic fervour. As the *Ladies Diary* theatre critic (1759) observed: 'It was with pleasure that I saw the heartfelt applause of the audience when the French valet, cook, and three French hairdressers were kicked off the stage in one of Mr Foote's farces at the now flourishing theatre at Covent Garden. I hope we shall follow in real life, and that this ridiculous people will have no more respect for them left in England, than in America.'

In the West Country more humane counsels prevailed. 'Letters from Bristol . . . report that there are upwards of one thousand, two hundred and forty poor French prisoners confined at Knowle . . . many of whom are destitute of clothing. It was decided to raise a subscription to provide some garments, and that a Committee be set up to manage the disposal of the money.'

Home-grown prisoners could fare less happily. The same journal reports: 'Thursday 22nd November 1759. Last Monday at half an hour after eight in the morning, John Ayliffe Esq., was carried from Newgate in an open cart to Tyburn, and between eleven and twelve was executed for forging a leaf in the name of the Right Honourable Henry Fox Esq., He was about thirty-six years of age . . . and of a very good family. The execution was conducted with decency, and by some accident the knot slipped from under his ear, so that he hung a considerable time longer than usual before he was cut down.'

Unnatural death could take more bizarre forms. For George III's subjects in the New World, Red Indians were more than a romp between television ads. As

Overseas Intelligence reported: 'On Sunday evening an express arrived in four days from the Cherokees . . . and from the Commanding Officers of Fort Loudoun and Prince George. We hear that the Upper Cherokees have stopt communications to Fort Loudoun, and have scalped and killed two of that garrison, and another white man. The passes are said to be strongly guarded by different parties of Indians. All the traders in the nation are arrived at Fort George, conducted thither in the night through the woods by some friendly Indians; but they have been obliged to leave most of their goods behind them.'

While women across the Atlantic faced torrid summers, freezing winters, the problems of feeding their families and dodging scalp-hunting, poison-arrow shooting Indians, the British Fair coped with matters 'of graver consideration'. Whether, for instance, 'to wear caps indoors'; or whether to wear them at all. One editor expounded: 'Though the graver considerations of health, decency and warmth have made the cap part of the female dress, yet we set out . . . that every woman looks best without one. Heaven forbid I should give colds to half my young acquaintance. The ladies accustomed to larger caps must not venture to make the change at once, they must pare them away by hair-breadths.'

Hair, as always, was a major preoccupation. 'We recommend to . . . ladies to let their hair grow . . . as it pleases. High foreheads were once esteemed . . . but not by persons of taste. Now they are quite unfashionable; they give an air of vacancy and folly, even to the most sensible of countenances. The tweezers, pumice-stone and burgandy pitch must be banished from the toilette of every woman of taste.'

Brunettes had come into their own since the early 1700s. As the *Ladies Guide* observed, 'Black hair is particularly useful in setting off the whiteness of neck and skin.' Keeping it dark could be achieved with a concoction of gum dye, myrtle, bay leaves and walnut peelings. 'But nothing is more ridiculous', readers are reminded, 'than to see a lady . . . with her forehead a fine purple that was only to have darkened her hair.'

Beauty patches were not only fashionable, they were useful for concealing 'the livid buttony pimple', and for revealing character. 'Common women stick little patches about their mouths; prudes upon their cheeks, and those little better than flirts, about their eyes. But the woman of taste places one large patch upon the temple, and a very little one near its edge.'

There were, of course, limits to what 'a woman of taste' might venture. 'I am afraid it will appear great ignorance if the account of the face be concluded without mention of paint. There is but one thing to be said about it—tis to be let alone. White glazes the face after a few weeks, and even red turns the skin yellow. If any one would see the fatal certainty of this, every public place shows them the fashionable prostitute. It is a miserable spectacle.'

Diamonds were, as always, a girl's best friend. 'With regards ear-rings, I say none are becoming, except diamonds. Of all necklaces, diamonds are incomparably the most becoming.'

Less fortunate girls could make do with 'a single row of large, round, white beads on a black ribband. A necklace or a very narrow ribband show what they affect to hide, and make the neck look long.'

Such ploys were strictly for the young. Narrow-eyed suspicion met the beauty-conscious older woman trying to make the best of her looks. 'I cannot think that a woman will be at pains with white paste and black pomatum to fill up the crowsfoot wrinkles and scatterings of grey hair, or will subject herself to the disgust of false teeth, false eyebrows, false plumpness and false colours, merely to have it said she is a good-looking woman for her age. I should be sorry to carry my suspicion to extremes, though perhaps what one sees, even at the best of parties, might warrant it!'

'There are a set of ladies in this town, and there are young men in abundance who are perfectly suited to the purpose of these ladies. . . . A clean room, a cheerful fire, *the name of visiting and tea* are sufficient inducements to these idle youths.'

'The generality of the other sex like best what comes easiest, and had rather . . . be courted than have the trouble of courting. This pitiful spirit, this wretched indolence in men gives all into the hands of our sex whom years have made cunning, and the decay of their beauty renders desperate, because men favour their ease more than their judgement.'

'Tea and sympathy' probably featured Josiah Wedgwood's Etruria pottery, introduced around 1790. And the recently introduced practice of numbering the houses in London's streets obviously helped the indolent young men find these dangerous, if ageing, syrens more easily.

While the *Ladies Guide* carried the occasional fashion note—informing its readers that 'the waist is short, the stays fashionably low this season'—it was *The Ladies Magazine or Entertaining Companion for the Fair Sex, for their Use and Entertainment* which carried the first regular fashion features. Including, presumably, news of the ribbed hose just invented by one Jeremiah Strutt. 'External appearance', its readers were told, 'is the first inlet to the treasures of the heart.'

Another 'inlet to the heart', remorselessly exploited by the Fair, was the introduction into England of the Pianoforte, around 1767. Along with 'interesting stories, novels, tales, and romances intended to confirm Chastity and recommend Virtue' women's magazines now listed and in some cases printed the music of 'popular songs and ballads'.

The editor of the *Ladies Magazine* meanwhile declared that: 'The minds of the female sex, when properly cultivated, are not inferior to those whose honour it is to be the protectors and instructors of the Fair.' He promises that 'Every topic conducive of inspiring the juvenile bosom with the love of Virtue, and the detestation of Vice . . . will find a place in this Repository.' He might have claimed with justifiable pride that among his illustrators was one William Blake. Having promised to present his readers with 'all the latest fashions' he proceeds with male inconsistency, to decry them. 'I must beg the ladies for pardon for making this attack upon . . . their toilette, their head-dress two feet tall, their dresses, their arms shoved up by ridiculous shoulder-straps, enormous facings of fur.'

'Ridiculous circumferences of circles' in dress are one thing. 'We may possibly without murmuring see the sex load themselves with ridiculous assortments of ornaments . . . enormous ruffs, scarves etc.' but 'painting a double layer of rouge is too serious. All the graces which are put on at the glass are never equivelent to those nature has poured on them with a profuse hand. Diamonds, embroidery, damask and satins are no additions to beauty. Beauty does not stand in need of cultivation' concludes this naive male.

Like many men bent on 'improving and instructing the weaker sex', this editor was possessed by the Grandmother syndrome, the conviction that at some time, a generation or so back, there had existed a race of perfect wives and mothers; paragons who 'kept to their homes and never ventured abroad without their husbands, never indulged in idleness or extravagance'.

'If women would recover that empire which they seem . . . to have lost, they must change their present method of living, and do what their grandmothers did before them . . . go often to church, and be well acquainted with their homes. Instead of an eternal round of pleasure, they should study economy, never prefer a splendid visiting day to the quiet of their husbands. They should follow the example of their grandmothers who fully apprehended that a woman's duty lies in making her husband easy.'

Sharing his indignation with the wicked ways of the world was a disillusioned young miss, 'lately vacated boarding school' where 'she had been taught to look upon virtue as the greatest beauty', only to find: '. . . on entering this mart of gaiety and pleasure that a depravity of manners, a licentious extravagance of dress and behaviour were almost universal; that virtue seemed ambitious of resembling vice, and vice glorious in the deformities which it had been used to hide. That libertines were not only allowed the company of, but even seemed welcomed by virtuous women!

'Were the maxims I learned at school true or false?' she asks, adding pathetically, 'If false, how have I been deceived!'

Almost equally chagrined was 'a young lady, . . . not yet eight and twenty', who took to task a young man who confessed 'that he preferred women of forty and over, to young, foolish girls'.

Foolishness in women or girls was not tolerated by *The Ladies Magazine*. If the Elizabethan woman was enjoined 'not to let her distaff be ydle' this editor was equally determined that her descendants' brains kept alert. Even cookery recipes were presented in riddles:

*Peach Cream Ices* 1. Two sea-fish. 2. A vowel, and what vagabonds do. 3. A disease pecular to fowls, and what women use. 4. Four-fifths of a gem, and the ocean. 5. Servitude. 6. Half of a hermit's retirement, and the Scots word for man. 7. A comedian and two-fifths of a tree. 8. A consonant, and part of the head.

After which, readers could tackle four pages of algebra, five pages of geometry, then relax with a story in French.

That the 'silly season' is no modern invention is witnessed by an item appearing in the Summer issue of 1759. Something funny, it seemed, happened on the way to the cellar . . .

'On Monday last, as Mr James Rigley, master of the Golden Lion, Barnstaple, was going to the cellar, he met with an odd incident. A large Norway rat, being curious to taste an oyster that opened as usual, at tide-time, having put his forefoot to catch the fish, the oyster immediately closed, and held the rat fast.' Mr Rigley, who knew a sales-gimmick when he saw one, 'brought them up from the kitchen, where several hundreds of people came to see them'. And presumably boosted his profits drinking to his, each other's, and possibly the king's health. They might even have sung the national anthem 'God Save the King', popularised by Henry Carey some fifteen years earlier in 1744.

*The Ladies Diary*, erupting into patriotic verse extolling the Queen, proclaimed:

Virtue and sense, with female softness joined,
All that subdues and captivates mankind
In Britain's Matchless Fair, resplendent shine,
They rule Love's Empire by a Right Divine,
Justly their Charms the astonished world admires,
When Royal Charlotte's Bright example fires.

'Astonished admiration' was the last sentiment felt by the editor of *The Ladies
Magazine*. Writing in a contemporary issue he exclaimed: 'These puffed up monarchs

with their mighty grandeur! It is the people that pay for the robes of the royal bride, for their feasts, their fireworks, the embroidery on the nuptial bed, and when the royal babe is born, every one of its cries is metormorphised into a new tax.'

It is unlikely that he sang Dr Arne's 'Rule Britannia', written in the same year, 1740, as Handel's Water Music, with the requisite jingoistic enthusiasm. 'War', he wrote, 'is an organised system of robbery and murder. No tongue can express, nor it is in the power of words to declare, neither can the heart conceive the plunder, rapine, murder, wretchedness and misery occasioned by these bloody wars.

'What can be said in defence of these permits for robbery and murder granted by regular governments? They hang a poor starving fellow for taking a lamb to assuage his hunger, and patronise thousands who sack and plunder inoffensive cities, rob industrious merchants, and kill them if they dare resist.'

Readers seeking less disquieting fare could always turn to the 'Answers to Queries and Paradoxical Problems' in *The Ladies Diary*, in which a would-be suitor is advised: 'The language of sincerity is doubtless the most effective language to gain a virtuous lady's heart. To convince her of an attachment on your part is the surest means to produce a real one on hers.'

Competition for readership inspired the now familiar 'free gifts'. In 1788 *The Ladies Magazine* tempted readers with 'a musical supplement containing a song by Mr Handel'. Later issues included 'A prey to tender anguish' by Mr Haydn, and 'An aria from Mr Mozart's Magic Flute'. In 1796 *The Lady's Pocket Magazine* presented readers with 'A Beautiful Print of Britannia', reminding them that: 'At this important period . . . when the fate of nations depends on the negotiations to be affected in Paris, the subject of this beautiful little print . . . impresses upon every susceptible mind the characteristic energies of our country . . . her invincible Navy, her personal magnanimity and fortitude, her matchless union in strength, beauty, intrepidity, mildness, wisdom and humanity.'

Published in 1790, and measuring six inches by four, and 'embellished' by exquisite colour plates, the same magazine announced itself as 'an elegant and entertaining companion for the Fair Sex'. Somewhat surprisingly, for so genteel an audience, one story begins:

'Hell and the devil!' exclaimed my father in a thundering voice. 'Here's the d - - - d dinner spoiled and Frank not come! It has been an hour waiting for him, and now the meat is roasted to a rag, and the vegetables boiled to a jelly.'

Such rantings were a male perogative. 'Delicacy' and 'sensibility' were the order of the day for heroines who, doomed, deathly pale, despairing, wronged, ruined, swooned their way through tear-drenched fiction.

'Edmund approached the bed and clasped her almost lifeless hand. . . . As the well-known voice vibrated in her ear, she opened her eyes. The sentence murmured on her lips. "Adieu my beloved father, and my long-mourned Edmund! Your cruel father forbade that we should love, but in heaven we shall meet again."

'Edmund flung himself beside the inanimate form of the hapless Helen, gazing wildly at her lifeless features, lovely, even in death.

"Ah Helen, my beloved Helen!" exclaimed the frantik youth—"All is fled with thee!" Then starting from the kneeling posture, and striking his burning forehead, he staggered and fell senseless to the floor.'

The traditionally British 'stiff upper-lip' was as yet unknown to these eighteenth-century heroes, whose affection for those of their own sex, then accepted unquestioningly, might today provoke a somewhat different reaction.

'Lord Henry could not speak to the mournful, though silent appeal in Wareham's eyes. He clasped him hastily to his heart and said in an agony of sorrow, "I am wretched! I must lose you! Good God, we must part!!" Henry folded him to his heart, almost suffocated with emotion, and breaking from him instantly, rushed precipitately to his cabin. . . . The picture of Wareham he had fastened to his neck . . . met his eyes, and he kissed it eagerly.'

'The tears rolled over his lovely face as he spoke. Wareham pressed Henry's hand gratefully to his lips. . . . A low sigh burst in sad unison from the bosom of each.'

'The feelings of Edwin overcame him. Flinging himself into the bosom of his friend, he pressed him strongly to his heart, while the scalding tears rained from his throbbing eyes.'

Other men clasped women to their bosoms. Not always with honourable intentions. Prostitution, a major problem, was not swept under the carpet by the *Ladies Magazine* fiction.

'Unhappy Maria! Little didst thou think when thou first listed under the banners of prostitution of the sorrows that awaited thee in the weary peregrination through the paths of sensuality. . . . Little didst thou imagine that all thy guilty pleasures would . . . terminate in infamy and disgrace. . . . These melancholy ejaculations were uttered by a young female who was standing near the Thames on the point of plunging into the stream.'

Another story finds the hero's curiosity aroused by a figure 'seated dejectedly on one of the benches' in the fashionable haunt of prostitutes, the Ranalagh Gardens.

'I paused . . . reflecting whether this appearance of sorrow could be effect or design. . . . My heart palpitated with an emotion for which I could not account . . . for I had reason to believe she was a girl of the town.

"Will no one take compassion on you, my dear?" said I . . . at the same time pressing her unreluctant hand.

"Compassion?" she repeated. "Compassion is not to be expected here. Yet if your heart is not totally destitute of sensibility, for pity's sake do not insult my distress."'

The heroine, as yet unsullied, is trying to save her elderly mother from starvation. The hero however, is unable to bring himself to marry a woman 'who had sunk so low'.

The campaigning editor of *The Ladies Magazine* directed his strictures elsewhere.

'Shall we court, fawn and attend like a gentleman usher, on vice in embroidery, while we loath, detest and consign to the gibbet without pity or remorse, the vice we behold in rags?

'Shall the unhappy female, driven by necessity, not lust, to the bitter, humiliating resource of prostitution, skulk in holes and corner, afraid of the beadle and his lash, while the dignified prostitute . . . confident of her protection, and honoured where she should be spurned, triumphs in her turpitude and insults neglected virtue with impunity?' Side-swipes perhaps at Harriet Wilson, the fashionable demi-monde who, on threatening to print the Duke of Wellington's love letters, occasioned the famous rejoinder 'Publish and be damned!' Or at Nelson's famous, or infamous mistress, Emma Hamilton?

Nelson's official correspondence provided frequent women's magazine copy. A letter written aboard the '*Agamemnon* off Loana' on 23 April 1796 'confided':

'This morning, having received information that a convoy laden with stores for the French Army had anchored off Loana, I lost no time in proceeding off that place . . .

'The vessels, lying very near the shore, a heavy fire of musquetry was kept on our boats, and it is with greatest grief I have to mention that Lieut. James Noble of the *Agamemnon*, a most valiant and gallant officer, is, I fear, mortally wounded. Signed, Horatio Nelson.'

A year previously, with commendable impartiality, *La Belle Assemblée* had published a letter written aboard *The Orient* on 22 June by an equally famous personage, Napoleon Bonaparte.

'Soldiers,

'You are going to undertake a conquest of which effects on civilisation, and the commerce of the world are incalculable.

'You will give to England the most certain . . . stroke, till you may be able to give her her death's stroke.

'We shall make fatiguing marches. We shall engage in several battles. We shall succeed in our enterprises. The fates are with us.

'The people among whom we are going to live are Mahometans. Their first article of faith is There is no other God but God, and Mahomet is his Prophet. Do not contradict them.

'The people to whom we are going treat women in a different manner than we do, but in every country he who ravishes is a monster.

'Pillage enriches only a few men, it dishonours, destroys our resources, it makes enemies of these people which it is in our interest to retain as friends.'

But if Britain ruled the waves, her record on land was more sombre. No women's magazine published during the 1914–18 or the 1939–45 wars presented its readers with anything comparable to the stark account carried by *The Ladies Magazine* during 1796, headed 'The Sufferings of the British Troops in the Retreat through Holland, 1795–6':

'The sickness of the Army increased daily with the extreme severity of the weather, and the total inattention to the comforts . . . of our suffering fellow-creatures rendered their situation pitiable in extreme.

'Invalids were . . . constantly sent to the hospital at Rhenen without any previous orders having been issued to prepare for their reception, so that no proper accomodation could be provided for them. They are usually conveyed in bilanders [small vessels employed to convey baggage] without even a sufficient supply of provisions.

'It is a notorious fact that . . . about five hundred miserable objects were embarked with only a single hospital-mate to attend them, with scarcely any covering, and with a scanty allowance of straw.

'They had not been expected and . . . there was no room at the hospital. A gentleman . . . declared that he himself one morning counted two and forty dead bodies on the banks of the river of men who had perished on board the bilanders because there was no quarters in the town.

'The enormous sum of forty-thousand pounds had been drawn to supply the sick with wine; and such was the infamous behaviour of the medical staff that the surgeon and his mates . . . many of them in the habit of robbing the sick, preferred the pleasure of carousing over flaggons . . . to the drudgery of alleviating the pangs of the afflicted patients whose hard fate placed them under such . . . inhuman butchers.

'A general order . . . for the removal of the sick proved a death warrant to numberless helpless and miserable objects. Constantly moved in open waggons, exposed to the severity of the weather, to drifting snow and heavy falls of sleet and rain, frequently without victuals . . . littered down in cold churches upon a short allowance of dirty straw, few enjoying the comforts of even a single blanket . . . it is no wonder they expired, martyrs to the most infamous and unpardonable neglect.'

The fate of the girls who refused to be 'left behind', wives, camp followers and their children, was no less harrowing.

'Owing to . . . the snow, which lying deep upon the ground was drifted in the faces of the men in a strong easterly wind, they were so worn down with fatigue . . . it was necessary to halt some of the regiments at two neighbouring villages.

'Numbers of men . . . and several women and children were frozen to death. An officer of the Guards was ordered to reconnoitre next morning. The distressing account . . . is given in his own words:

'On the morning of the 17th I was sent . . . to trace a road . . . by which the army might safely proceed to Loonen. . . . It was scarcely light, and as the day broke, the horrible scene it revealed afforded a shocking proof of the miseries of the winter's campaign.

'About a half a mile left of the high road we discovered a baggage cart . . . apparently in distress. I galloped to the spot, and found the poor animals were stiff but not dead; the hoar-frost on their manes showing they had been there all night. Not perceiving any driver, I struck my sword repeatedly upon the canvas. . . . At length a feeble voice answered. . . . A pair of naked, frost-nipped legs was then advanced, and the most miserable object I ever beheld sunk heavily upon the ground, the whole of his cloathing so ragged . . . I can scarcely say he was covered. So stiff and frozen . . . that he was by no means capable of moving.

'He informed me that his regiment . . . had lost its road, and in turning into another, he found his horses incapable of clearing the cart from the ruts, and that himself and two comrades were left behind to preceed in the best manner they could. The two men he spoke of were lying dead in the cart.

'The whole of this day's march was marked by scenes of a calamitious nature. We could not proceed a hundred yards without perceiving the dead bodies of men, women and children and horses.

'Near another cart we perceived . . . a beautiful young woman with an infant . . . at the breast, both frozen to death. The mother had expired in the act of suckling her child as, one breast exposed, she lay upon the drifting snow; the milk in a stream drawn from the nipple by the babe, and instantly congealed. The infant, its little head upon its mother's bosom, with an overflow of milk frozen as it trickled from its mouth.'

Inexplicably, the Napoleonic wars (1793–1815) featured little in contemporary fiction. Instead, Horace Walpole's novel, *The Castle of Otranto* (1764) established a vogue for the Gothic not unlike today's. No women's magazine was complete without its quota of ghostly abbeys, lonely castles, secret passages, chests filled with rotting bones, haunted caskets, eerie towers, violent storms, unearthly groans, gaping tombs, caves, dungeons, shrieks, 'horrid phantoms'. Heroes were named Ranaldo, Alphonso, Bernardo. Villains were likely to be called Jasper. Jane Austen's *Northanger Abbey* was a glorious send-up of the genre.

In 'De Courville Castle, A romance by a young lady', Alphonso, the hero, finds his father's supposed murderer languishing in a dungeon:

'Alphonso was much agitated. . . . He raised the man from the ground . . . and removing the hair which covered his face discovered the peasant . . . and murderer of his father. "Villain!" (exclaimed he, while every joint trembled with emotion) "Vengeance is now within my reach! Prepare to expiate thy crimes. In me behold the injured Alphonso!" . . . The man sprang forward and averted the stroke. "Hold, hold, I conjure you!" (he cried frantikly) "I am not the monster you suppose me. . . . My guilty story must not be revealed at present. . . . All I dare say is . . . your father lives!"'

By contrast, short terse paragraphs reported the murder and mayhem of the world outside. 'The Register of Remarkable Occurrences during the year 1796' (*Ladies Magazine*) records:

'January 1st. British troops engaged in the unsuccessful expedition to the coast of France, returned to Portsmouth.

'An armistice was concluded upon the Rhine after desparate fighting, by which both armies were rendered incapable of continuing the combat.

'Several depradations and acts of violence committed by the Orange Boys of the North of Ireland against the Roman Catholic inhabitants.

'General Bonaparte, Commander in Chief of the French Army in Italy, has completely defeated the Austrian and Sardinian troops . . . with the loss of fourteen thousand, five hundred men.'

Some disputes were nearer home:

'On Sunday morning, between five and six oclock, Mr Carpenter and Mr Pride, two American young gentlemen . . . went to Hyde Park to settle an affair of Honour.

'The meeting took place in consequence of the affairs of America becoming the subject of conversation at the Virginia Coffee House on Saturday night. Mr Carpenter gave it as his opinion that Mr Giles, a member of the Congress of the United States, was not . . . politically honest.

'At this observation Mr Pride took offence, and a challenge ensued. The distance being measured they fired exactly at the same instance, when Mr Carpenter received his antagonist's ball in his side; and though he was conveyed immediately in a Hackney coach to Richardson's hotel, and the ball extracted, he died on Monday.'

Blowing one's political top via a 'letter to the Editor' was less hazardous. In the same issue an irate Papa complains:

'Sir, My giddy and inconsiderate girls who so far from supporting the M.P. who has long and respectably catered for us . . . excited by the democratic party . . . now boldly face the populace, shake hands with the lowest, and most profligate, in my presence, have submitted to be saluted [kissed] in order to gain votes!'

'The participation of women in politics . . . without offending against delicacy or propriety' likewise perplexed the editor of *The Ladies Monthly Magazine or Cabinet of Fashion* (1790). It was, he conceded, 'acceptable for them to know enough to impress the tender minds of their children with the rudiments of constitutional principles . . . and occasionally to contribute to male conversation.' Throwing a light upon the contemporary scene, he adds: 'While I admit the propriety of women being politicians so far, I am unwilling to allow them the privilege of being partisans in elections, and of bustling among a riotous and drunken mob who are sinking themselves to the level of beasts while they pretend to support the interest of some popular candidate.'

'Rebellion', new thinking, was in the air. In 1790 Edmund Burke wrote his *Reflections on the French Revolution*. William Blake enlarged on the theme in 1791, challenged orthodox views on marriage, and authority. In the same year Tom Paine wrote *The Rights of Man*. And a year later Mary Wollstoncraft published her *Vindication of the Rights of Women*—then thought outrageous. Robert Emmet and Wolfe Tone preached independence in Ireland. The Slave Trade had recently been abolished. Scottish miners were freed from serfdom.

The wars, and inevitably, increased taxation, raged on, arousing in at least one correspondent of *The Ladies Magazine* 1796 a confused mixture of protest and patriotism.

'Sir, It is impossible for an educated man like myself to fill up the papers now circulated for the property and assessed taxes, without having to recourse to the Law; and it is almost as difficult to avoid error in making returns as to find money to pay for the contributions imposed on us for the necessities of State, owing to the turbulence of our neighbour, *Boney*. But that is neither here nor there; we must fight it out, and pay it out, as long as we have money, blood and spirit!'

While such men 'fought it out'—largely, one suspects, from fireside chairs and the pages of women's magazines, the younger and abler, persuaded by family tradition, 'honour', unemployment, the recruiting sergeant's shilling, or the press gangs, marched away to that very apt 'pop song' of the day—'The girl I left behind me'.

Music of a different order perturbed the magazine editors. Recently introduced from Vienna was that shocking innovation—'destined to corrupt the morals of the young'—the waltz. 'The couples', it was reported, 'hold each other at arm's length and gyrate about each other in a most stupid fashion. It is a ridiculous dance and none but the very young should attempt it.'

Worry as they might about their daughters waltzing, chasing Red Coats, making or failing to make suitable matches, the axiom that wisdom and authority was vested in parents rather than in their teenage children, went unquestioned. Young girls were cautioned: 'If your Papa or Mama should at any time express disapprobation of your conduct . . . resolve to amend it. Apologise for your past, and promise for the future to offend no further. Be sure to avoid all pert or self-sufficient replies . . . sullen looks and dumb resentment. Obey your parents' wishes, and you will offend neither delicacy or propriety.' (*Ladies Magazine* 1792).

War or no, knowing what to wear, when, remained important. Fashion notes included:

*Morning dress for February*: 'Nightcap of fpotted muflin, trimmed with a double border of lace . . . bound with a narrow maroon ribband, tied with a fmall bow in front; hat covered with blue fatin, tied under the chin, and trimmed with blue and maroon striped ribbands. Round gown of falmon-coloured flowered chintz; long sleeves, fur muff.'

*Afternoon dress*: 'An Armenian turban of . . . flamed-coloured fatin, croffed in front with two strings of pearls and the ends trimmed with a gold fringe. A white ostrich and blue efprit feather on the left side. Armenian robe of embroidered muflin. . . . Two strings of pearls and feftoon gold chains with medallion round the neck. Hair dressed in light curls and ringlets.'

Such grand ladies had merely to step into their carriages or sedan chairs (introduced into England around 1581). For lesser women there could be problems. In a feature 'The Miseries of Human Life' *The Ladies Monthly Magazine* records:

'Going out to dinner: no coach, dirty streets; silk stockings; following on tip-toe a short, fat woman in pattens along a crowded way, anxiously hoping every minute to pass her, when she suddenly stops to hitch on her patten, the sharp rim of which violently grates your instep, already sore from a previous incident.'

Propitiating the male was as vital as ever, though sometimes 'the Fair' retaliated. While an earlier correspondent had protested against a young man's preference for 'women of forty and over' a correspondent of *The Ladies Magazine* of 1796 challenged a contrary view.

'Gentlemen, You have said that ladies between thirty and forty are old women! A charge so atrocious. . . . I am at loss for words to express the barbarity of it.

'If such an abominable doctrine was once believed it would . . . send the loveliest of our sex to an untimely grave. Their husbands . . . will go astray in search of young women in the nurseries and baby houses.' The letter was signed, 'Matura'.

This edition also carried a tongue-in-cheek series of articles 'Remarks on the Education of Females in England' purporting to come from a 'Hindoo Rajah'.

'During infancy these Christian females . . . receive their first ideas from mercenary attendants, always ignorant and frequently vicious.

'Lest from the conversation of fathers and brothers these young females might . . . acquire some degree of information, they are removed . . . and placed where science, reason and commonsense dare not intrude. In these seminaries their time is employed in learning a few tricks, such as a monkey might acquire, called accomplishments'.

'Another indispensable part in the education of females . . . is the tongue spoken in their neighbour nation. . . . After many conjectures I formed the belief that as the French nation was frequently at war with England it might be customary to send women hircarrahs [spies] into the camp of the enemy. . . . I was however forced to give up this conclusion on being assured that after years spent in the study of this language, few are capable of . . . conversing with any degree of fluency in this tongue . . . the only advantage resulting from it was that they were enabled to understand the peculiar terms belonging to the articles of dress imported from that country which has an acknowledged right of imposing its fashions on the other nations of Europe.'

# CHAPTER THREE

# *Competitors*

THE year 1801 saw England's red and white cross of St George unite with Scotland's blue and white banner of St Andrew and Ireland's cross of St Patrick to form the first Union Jack.

In France, a year later, Napoleon Bonaparte 'the Corsican monster' was elected First Consul. Beethoven was composing in Vienna. In Wales, a Cornishman named Trevethick experimented with the first steam-train.

'The renewal of war with France' went largely unremarked in women's magazines. Only the death of Nelson reversed the entrenched conviction that 'politics and war' were 'indelicate subjects beyond women's mental scope'. As the editor of *The Ladies Monthly Museum or Polite Repository of Amusement and Instruction, being an assemblance of whatever can tend to please the fancy, interest the Mind or exalt the Character of the British Fair* explained, in the January issue of 1806:

'No one has a more decided aversion to the character of petticoat politicians than myself; even where the *understanding* is male, the *delicacy* of the female should be preserved.

'Nor could I ever see why . . . it is thought a compliment of the men to exclude political subjects in the company of ladies; and an equal courtesy for women to . . . leave important topics to men.

'I am led to these considerations by a subject that has taken full possession of me. How should it be otherwise when that great and exalted bulwark of his country, Admiral Nelson . . . is . . . passing from his watery bier to the beloved shore he has so long and nobly defended.'

*La Belle Assemblée*, published by John Bell in 1790, 'A Fashionable Magazine addressed particularly to The Ladies', cashed in on the hero's death with a special edition which sold over fourteen thousand copies.

Of more intimate concern to women was the recently introduced Circassion Corset, named after 'the favourite companion' of the Persian Ambassador, and marketed by Mrs M. A. Bell. A shrewd business woman, she combined the roles of fashion-writer for *La Belle Assemblée*, with proprietress of gown-shops in Bloomsbury and St James 'patronised by Her Royal Highness, the Duchess of Kent'.

'The new corset' she wrote, 'gives the form that ease and gracefulness which supports of steel and whalebone inevitably destroy. It displays without indelicacy the shape of the bosom to the greatest possible advantage.

Frontispiece of *The Family Economist*, 1850, a penny monthly with a mission to the Home, determined to 'remove its discomforts and enhance its pleasures' especially for those 'hundreds of thousands' who were 'most wretched and miserable'.

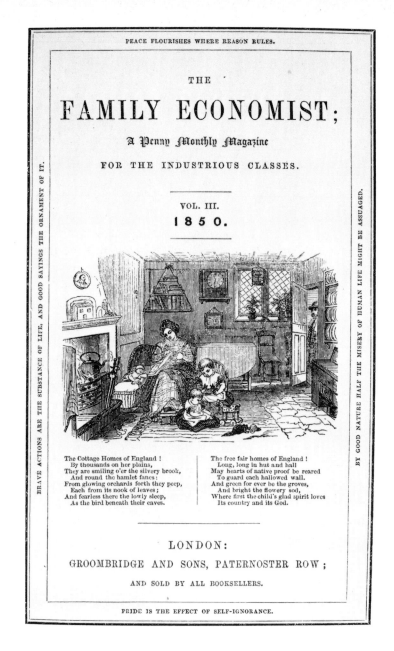

PEACE FLOURISHES WHERE REASON RULES.

THE
# FAMILY ECONOMIST;
𝔄 𝔓𝔢𝔫𝔫𝔶 𝔐𝔬𝔫𝔱𝔥𝔩𝔶 𝔐𝔞𝔤𝔞𝔷𝔦𝔫𝔢
FOR THE INDUSTRIOUS CLASSES.

VOL. III.
1850.

BRAVE ACTIONS ARE THE SUBSTANCE OF LIFE, AND GOOD SAYINGS THE ORNAMENT OF IT.

BY GOOD NATURE HALF THE MISERY OF HUMAN LIFE MIGHT BE ASSUAGED.

The Cottage Homes of England !
By thousands on her plains,
They are smiling o'er the silvery brook,
And round the hamlet fanes:
From glowing orchards forth they peep,
Each from its nook of leaves;
And fearless there the lowly sleep,
As the bird beneath their eaves.

The free fair homes of England !
Long, long in hut and hall
May hearts of native proof be reared
To guard each hallowed wall.
And green for ever be the groves,
And bright the flowery sod,
Where first the child's glad spirit loves
Its country and its God.

LONDON:
GROOMBRIDGE AND SONS, PATERNOSTER ROW;
AND SOLD BY ALL BOOKSELLERS.

PRIDE IS THE EFFECT OF SELF-IGNORANCE.

'Of all the charms which embellish, the bosom is indisputably that which addresses itself in the strongest terms to the senses which most powerfully excite the passion of love. A woman proud of her beauty may be nothing but a coquette; One who makes a display of her bosom is something more; she wishes to inflame the senses and make a speedy victory.'

Whether or not allured by such 'embellishments' Lord Byron was making his own 'speedy victories' in bed, and in print. But not with the approval of the *Ladies Magazine*'s literary critic. 'The poem, Childe Harold's Pilgrimage' he observed, 'is reminiscent of a Methodist Class meeting, where the greatest sinner obtains the highest honours.'

Like the Elizabethans, and ourselves during the Second World War, the Georgians lived under the threat of invasion. Locally recruited militia were stationed on the south coast. Martello towers dotted the shore from Folkestone in Kent to Seaford in Essex. But it was a different 'invasion' which infuriated a gentlemen who in these decimalised, litred, kilometred days must be whizzing in his grave. In 1807 he wrote to *The Lady's Monthly Magazine or Polite Repository of Amusement and Instruction*:

'Mr Editor, I am an an old-fashioned mortal known by the name of T R U E E N G L I S H M A N; a plain speaker, a lover of beef and an abominator of foreign customs. The invasion of French *men* I value not a rush. We are ready! But I must confess there is another species of invasion which vexes me exceedingly. I mean the confounded custom of introducing *French words* into our language, which is arrived to such a height that a plain country gentleman can scarcely understand one word in ten of his *mother-tongue*; it is frittered away by what our sailors call puppy-lingo.

'One man, at a loss to explain himself, comes out with "*Je ne sais quoi*". A second, won't describe particulars but praises "*le tout ensemble*". A third drops in when dinner is serving up and declares he comes "*a propos*". A fourth cannot enter a theatre without exclaiming, "*What a coup d'oeil!*". A fifth vows that Mrs —— is not handsome, but her face has a pleasing "*tourure*". A sixth sagaciously doubts whether a minister is "*au fait*".

'I don't find fault with certain women being styled *elegantes*, simpering misses, *belles*, and effeminate fellows *beaux*, but I am transported with rage when I reflect that this unaccountable innovation has even crept into our Army.

'Our soldiers are instructed to *deployer a feu de joye*, while our Volunteer Associations are universally called *Corps*.

'Excuse my wrath, Mr Editor, and allow your circulating Museum to be the vehicle of an attempt to dissuade my brave countrymen *from uttering the sentiments of Britons with the tongues of Frenchmen*.

'I am, Mr Editor,
Your Humble Servant and a
T R U E   E N G L I S H M A N.'

In her autobiography *Millions Made my Story*, Mary Grieve, editor of *Woman* from 1938–62 stated, 'It is of the first importance that the reader should see her own life reflected in the pages, and not that of some luckier, richer, cleverer creature', a sentiment anticipated by 'A Father of Two Girls' writing to *The Ladies Magazine* in 1806.

'This magazine', he objects, 'is more inclined to give us an account of fashionable folks, and to write for the gay world, than for the persons of middling rank in life.

'Now I consider this a defect . . . for the former are too wise to take advice from their inferiors, and those who would be glad to listen to you do not often come in for any share of your notice.

'To nine-tenths of the world it is of very little consequence what is going on at public places, and how routes and balls are conducted; but all have an interest in virtuous principles, frugal manners, and advice and instruction on persons in our walk of life.

'We have the same right to that which suits us for our money, as the great and gay. Silks and muslins are less necessary stuffs than calicoes, and . . . grand doings are little interesting or useful to those who are to labour for a living, or . . . to take care to spend with economy what others earn by diligence.

'I have ever thought it of more consequence to make young people good, sober, diligent and saving, than to make them accomplished.

'Signed: Plain Gloucestershire Yeoman.'

To which the editor replies, promising 'Henceforth the magazine will endeavour now and then, to visit the cottage and the farmhouse . . . as well as the abodes of fashion and elegance. Perhaps the Fair Reader will have no objection by way of a change, to sit down to homely fare, which will give a higher relish to those delicacies that they are more accustomed to.'

Like its predecessors and successors, *The Ladies Monthly Museum* carried its Questions and Answers feature. These featured queries between 'Lydia Quisitive' and 'a paragon of ancient matrons, a fountain-head of wisdom' writing under the unflattering pseudonym, 'Old Woman'. Questions included:

Q. When should a girl be out of leading strings, or when may she answer for herself without referring backwards and forwards to Mama?

A. When she has the prudence to walk alone, and can be satisfied in her heart and conscience that she owes no further duty to the author of her being, and the guide of her youth.

Q. If a girl has half-a-dozen admirers, and feels no partial attachment for any, is she to run the risk of losing them all by rejecting their suits . . . or is she to keep them all in hope till she finds how her heart will decide?

A. None but a coquette can ever be in such a predicament.

Today's fears that television 'corrupts the young' equates with the nineteenth century's apprehension about 'the evils of novel reading'. 'This kind of reading ought certainly to be restrained, if not prohibited', declares *The Ladies Monthly Museum* (1807). 'Those engaged in the selection of books for young people cannot be too careful in the examination of novels, as the worst principles may sometimes be discovered in a most dangerous and artful form.'

It was a predicament that faced a distraught father visiting a Spa—'those nurseries of intrigue, and passports to ruin, that sinful place, Bath'—in search of a cure for his wife. He explains to the editor:

'As our daughters, aged nineteen and twenty, had been virtuously brought up, I could not imagine that any danger would be apprehended in carrying them along with us as a solace to their mother.

'In order that my daughters might have something rational to amuse them, I called at one of those magazines of poison, vulgarly called Circulating Libraries.'

Having chosen books 'calculated to beautify and inform their minds' he found to his dismay that their maid-servant 'a giddy girl' had 'procured other books . . . and it appeared that my Sarah and Sukey . . . devoured them with avidity for a long time, unknown to me'.

Worse was to follow.

'I had not been away on business three days till that wench of a servant . . . lured them into what is called a Playhouse; and though they must at first have felt horror at entering such a receptacle of folly and irreverence, novelty, it appears, engaged their attention. They repeated this sinful practice, and one of the gay fellows who wore a cockade in the King's Livery, ventured to address Sukey . . . and after paying her some extravagent compliments . . . prevailed with them next day to walk around the public haunts of dissipation they had never visited before. He even had the artifice to engage one of his comrades to lend his arm to Sarah, that he might have the ear of her sister to himself!

'Providence, it seemed, ordered that I should come to their rescue. Forgetful of their duty to God, and their fond parents, and flattered out of their reason, they had consented to take an excursion in a carriage with their admirers, when I unexpectedly, hastening on the wings of affection . . . met them on the road, and rescued them from their insidious destroyers.'

Erring sons could equally provoke parental headaches. A father, visiting his seventeen year old apprentice son unexpectedly, in London, records:

'I found him at his lodgings, far from well, reclining in an easy chair, while a young woman stood over him, applying sal volatile salts.

' "My father!" he articulated, in feeble accents. I fondly pressed him to my throbbing heart, whilst tears supplied the place of language.

'The young woman, whom I had scarcely perceived, remained transfixed to the spot . . . my eyes glanced over her person, which too fatally told a *melancholy truth*. I gave Edward a look, which he instantly comprehended, and turning towards the object of his illicit passion . . . required her to retire. A groan of anguish burst from his labouring bosom . . . and shading his face with his hands he burst into a violent flood of tears.

' "Your *penitence* would disarm *resentment*, if your situation did not excite compassion, my dear Edward," said I, withdrawing a hand which concealed his pallid face, and at the same time pressed it to my bosom with that warmth of impression which parental tenderness inspired.

' "Oh my father! I am unworthy of this proof of tenderness! I merited *reproaches*, and these I could have borne; but to receive such *unexampled marks of affection* . . . makes me doubly feel the iniquity of my conduct; yet I was not the seducer of this unfortunate girl."

'This declaration, Mr Editor, relieved my mind of a load of misery, for seduction always appeared to me as the most *henious of crimes*.' Nonetheless, egged on by this 'seductress' Edward becomes 'hopelessly in debt', and 'dies in an agony of shame', over which his father prefers 'to draw a veil'.

The more things change . . . 'There has, during the last few months, been an *enormous* advance on the cost of almost all the common necessaries of life. We take in . . . a loaf from the baker's cart . . . for which we have to pay elevenpence; last spring a loaf of the same weight cost only sixpence. . . . Butter too is dearer . . . currants more than double the price they were two years ago'. *The Family Economist*, 1854. (Photograph by Geoff Mayor.)

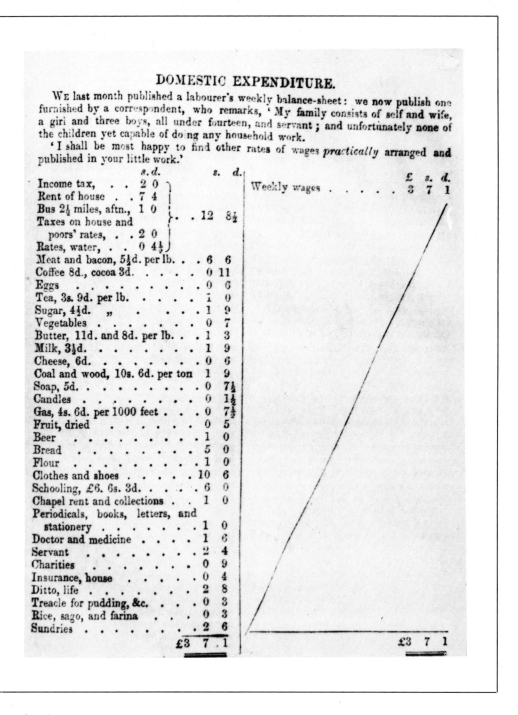

Judged almost as sinful as seduction, was 'a love of finery'. And who better to expose as an example than 'that haggard adultress', that 'wanton consort of the Corsican Ogre', Josephine La Pagerie, living it up across the Channel? *The Lady's Museum* of 1807 reveals:

'The extravagance of this wretched woman is equalled only by her wickedness! According to a respectable French periodical . . . she never puts on any plain gown twice, and changes her dress four or six times a day.

'In Summer she makes use of four dozen silk stockings, and three dozen of gloves and shoes; and in Winter, three dozen of the best English cotton stockings, and two dozen of French silk stockings *every week*. . . . All her chemises are of the finest cambrics, with borders of lace. Six dozen chemises with lace are made up for her *every month*.

'Every three months she exchanges her diamonds and jewels, or has them newly set according to the prevalent fashion. Four times in the year, her plate, china, furniture, tapestry hangings, carpets etc. are changed, according to the seasons. She has . . . two new carriages and twelve different horses every month.

'Twelve times in the year, all persons belonging to her household receive new accoutrements or liveries.'

If further proof of her depravity was needed, it had only to be added that the wanton creature took '*scented baths*'!

'By touching certain springs she can command what perfume her caprice demands. . . . By touching other springs she commands . . . drawings or pictures, elegant or voluptuous, gay or libertine as her fancy desires. At the signal of a bell, she is, by mechanical invention, lifted from the bathing machine into an elegant, moderately warm perfumed bed, where she is dried in two minutes; from which she is again lifted and laid down on a splendid sofa.'

Gleefully the writer continues: 'Although equally adored by her husband and the French Republic, Madame Napoleon has numerous family misfortunes'—the chief of these being, it seemed, the dislike of her sister-in-law.

'Her sister-in-law, the Princess Borghese . . . is an intolerable mimic of her juvenile airs, gait and dress, contrasted with her antique wrinkles, plump person, and worn-out voice. Such is this woman, who having given loose to her passions, deserves to be exhibited both as a shame to herself, and a warning to others whom future revolutions may tempt to imitation and degradation.'

That ugly, wrinkled, croaky-voiced, plump and depraved old Josephine was still adored by her dishy husband and notoriously volatile subjects, speaks volumes for qualities editorially commended elsewhere in the same issue: 'It is observable that women who have no pretensions to beauty are uncommonly accomplished and agreeable. Those who have natural good sense and energy of character are at pains to exert the one, and cultivate the other; and become more estimable, and often more esteemed than the beautiful women who rely on their beauty alone.'

Yet neither beauty nor estimable qualities were always proof against the duplicity of the fickle male, as one of that sex admits.

'When I look round me and behold the dreadful consequence which usually results from the duplicity and infidelity of my own sex,' he writes in an issue of this magazine, 'I cannot but sincerely wish that female rights were better supported.

'A man may now, with impunity, amuse himself by trifling with the feelings of an amiable and too credulous woman, whose sensibility and gratitude is ever excited by the smallest appearance of regard on our side; and after years of pointed attentions, during which timidity or delicacy may have prevented her from demanding a proper explanation, he changes the object of his pursuit, and feels himself fully acquitted by the satisfactory consolation of declaring *upon honour* he "never promised to marry the foolish girl". While the unhappy object of his pretended preference is left exposed to the malicious sneers of her enemies, the torturing pity of her friends and the painful conflicts of wounded pride and disappointed affection.'

It was a point poignantly underlined by a later correspondent:

'Nature has made woman weak that she may receive with gratitude the protection of man. Yet how often is this appointment perverted! How often does her protector become her oppressor! She may reject, but cannot invite, may tell what would make her wretched, but dare not even whisper what would make her happy, and in a word, exercise a negative upon the most important event in her life.

'Man has the leisure to look about him and marry at any age, but woman must improve the fleeting moment and determine quickly at the hazard of determining rashly. The springtime of her beauty will not last. Its wane will be the signal for the flight of her lovers, and if the present opportunity is neglected, she may be left to experience the only species of misfortune for which the world shows no sympathy.'

Even in the 'springtime of beauty', dangers 'could lurk unseen'. Particularly for girls who 'thought for themselves'. 'Advice to Young Ladies' reads: 'Yours is a truly amiable lot. Oh, be careful to preserve the privileges you possess. They are estimable, if rightly used; they will be fraught with ruin if neglected! Do not imagine . . . because the path you are treading seems smooth . . . that no danger lurks unseen, and that you are capable without assistance of avoiding them. . . . *If you reject the counsels of your parents* and begin too soon to think and act for yourselves, you will infallibly forfeit all the advantages you possess, and involve your future in a life of misery.'

Nor were mothers or even grandmothers 'sinking into the vale of years' always beyond reproach. 'We frequently see age ape-ing youth, and without the excuse of temptation, being obstinately peverse. We see mothers and grandmothers affecting to be thought handsome, dressing like girls, and covering their wrinkles with paint. We see them haunting places of public amusement and forgetting their private duties; and in short, setting an ill example to those they are bound to caution and direct.'

Red Coats not only unsettled the women, they inspired *Records of Weekly Amusements for the Fair Sex* with what was probably the biggest sales gimmick of all time. This periodical, 'designed to promote a love of virtue, with insinuating examples and diverting passages' dated back to 1710, and was the first women's magazine to serialise fiction. It now offered 'disconsolate damsels left lonely by the wars [Peninsular Wars 1808–14] a matrimonial lottery of ten thousand officers, single men, handsome and vigorous' with tickets at five pounds each. Unfortunately, no record exists of the outcome.

40

'Disconsoling' as they were to damsels, the wars brought some satisfaction to the editor of *The Ladies Monthly Museum*. They discouraged foreign travel. 'Notwithstanding the benefits which travel abroad is calculated to convey ... numbers have their natural feelings perverted and imbibe notions incompatible with their happiness and duty, from visiting foreign lands. . . . It strikes me therefore, as a fortunate circumstance for our patrician youth, that their manners have neither been corrupted, nor their sentiments warped of late years, by foreign travel; the state of the Continent being such, that they have been . . . obliged to confine themselves to home travels.'

The Fair Sex, especially, could 'reap sufficient knowledge of foreign countries from reading of travels; such books I earnestly recommend in preference to insipid novels and ridiculous romances.'

Not that this editor objected to 'an occasional sojourn at a public place, provided the heart is guarded against the frivolity and extravagance which are too frequently inmates of such haunts'. Trendiest among these places, as Jane Austen's last, unfinished novel, *Sanditon* witnesses, were the newly fashionable seaside resorts. As William Cowper expressed it:

> Now widow, virgin, wife
> Ingenious to diversify dull life,
> In coaches, chaises, caravans and hoys,
> Fly to the coast for daily, nightly joys,
> And all impatient of dry land, agree
> With one consent to rush into the sea.

*La Belle Assemblée* records, 'Some of those distinguished Summer resorts called Watering places are now grown into so much importance that dispatches appear in public journals from those seats of pleasure with far more regularity than those from seats of war.'

Along with the 'wicked Spas' and the 'dissipated City' such places encouraged absentee landlords 'to leave unlimited power in the hands of unfeeling stewards whose private interests rise from oppression' while they (the landlords) 'indulged in a vortex of gaiety'. Eventually, after 'too free an expenditure' they return to their ancestral seats:

> There, hid in loathed obscurity, removed
> From pleasure, left but never more beloved,
> Yet just endures, and with a sickly spleen
> Sighs o'er the beauties of the charming scene;
> He likes the country, but in truth must own,
> Most likes it when he studies it from town.

But the evils of Continental travel, the pitfalls of the Watering Places, even the vices of the town, were as nothing compared with 'the folly, credulousness and avarice which activates emigration to the New World'. Today's admiration for those

Emigration with its attendant partings, sorrows and life-long separations was a constant theme in Victorian life and fiction. Illustration from *The Family Friend*. Eleanor Archer Collection, by courtesy of Warwick Museum Service.

No. 117.

# THE FAMILY FRIEND.

GRACE BIDDING FAREWELL TO HER BROTHER ARTHUR.

p. 134

September, '79.

One Penny.

valiant pioneers braving the unknown, facing incredible odds, overcoming seemingly unendurable hardships, was not shared by *La Belle Assemblée*'s editor.

'Those emigrants are of a roving disposition . . . in search of new frivolities . . . this is the great cause of the perpetual influx of foreigners into the United States.

'Thousands have been lured thither by false statements and delusive hopes; numbers fled with money of their creditors, or to avoid the punishment which the Law was preparing to inflict. . . . Amongst these . . . classes of people have been many who detest the restraints of civilised society . . . to whom the unrestrained life of savages appears delightful. Such for the most part are the backwoodsmen who fell the first trees, erect miserable hovels.

'When one . . . of industrious habits becomes the proprietor, he begins to clear the land . . . or build a more commodious house. These habitations . . . are either log or framed houses. The roof is generally of bark. The chimney, if there be any, is a pile of stones; if not, a fire is made on the ground and a hole left in the roof to emit smoke.

'In every season a constant fire must be kept . . . to keep off the mosquitoes and other insects . . . and the same precaution . . . taken to defend the cattle from them; as smarting under the venom of these insects they will disappear into the forests and grow wild. A smouldering fire of green leaves and brushwood will cause a great smoke . . . nothing could be imagined more dreary.' Or, less 'frivolous'.

'The European emigrant . . . who has witnessed a different order of things, is prey to chagrin, disappointment and despair . . . and vegetates where his folly, credulity and avarice has placed him. His children . . . are reconciled to their fate. One generation suffices to convert the European into an American.'

The women who went with their men to these 'outlandish' shores, needed a generous share of 'conjugal affection' a topic ever-dear to the heart of *The Lady's Monthly* editor (1807). 'It is a common, but mistaken notion', he wrote, 'which too many females entertain, particularly after they become wives, that if they adhere to the precepts of virtue . . . they need not study to render themselves further amiable. Simply to practise commonplace virtue will never win or maintain an empire over the heart. Even beauty and virtue united, are too weak to bind the affections without good sense and good temper. Good sense and good temper, ordinary features enlivened by good humour, and set off by mental charms, will in the end prevail over all the transient witcheries of corporeal form.'

Such 'witcheries of corporeal form' spelled ruin for Annette, 'a sweet village girl' and heroine of a story (in this issue), who caught the lecherous eye of the Lord of the Manor's 'dissipated' son. Her spurned sweetheart, 'hearing her name coupled with dishonour', drowns himself. Her mother 'raves and tears her hair'. Annette, 'red-eyed with weeping' goes mad.

Emphasising the moral, 'a regular reader' confesses how 'beauty, combined with a headstrong nature . . . brought her to the folly of a headstrong marriage. I would tell the young and heedless of my sex' she warns, 'that without duty to parents and a submissive attention to husbands, they can never expect to be happy in any condition of life.'

Precept was one thing; practice, another. 'A bachelor's observations', in an 1818 issue of *La Belle Assemblée*, record a 'conjugal exchange' between a wife, 'she but one and twenty', and her husband 'he, twenty-eight, and married but six weeks' which would not have met with the approval of the editor of the *Ladies Monthly Museum*. The husband complains as dinner is served that 'she knew he detested rabbits fried'.

' "That is excellent!" retorted the lady. "It was but last Thursday you declared you liked them fried on account of the crisped parsley of which you were particularly fond!"

' "Why, I never eat crisped parsley, my dear Amelia!" That was pronounced with a satiric grin, which seemed to convert "my dear" into "my devil". The lady appeared to understand, for she exclaimed: "I'm sure if I study your appetite from June to January, no dish would please. Heigh ho! I wish I had never married. All men are alike. All kindness before the ceremony. All ill-humour afterwards." ' And when her husband drinks to 'Your reformation, Madame!' she responds in like tone to 'the removal of your ill-humour, my sweet, irritable Sir!' making her husband a profound bow.

Such behaviour, editors agreed, was a modern phenomenon. As *The Lady's Magazine*, 1818, expounding on 'The Propriety of Conduct to be observed by Married and Unmarried women' exclaimed: 'The prevalence of Vice, which in former ages was considered a rare instance of human depravity, now affords a perpetual subject for discussion in Doctor's Commons.' 'Laxity of principles, and an erroneous method of education' were blamed. 'Male and female are as indiscriminately blended as if they were intended to follow the same pursuits. *There are instances of young females who display as much freedom in the society of the opposite sex, as they do in their own.*' For 'the alarming increase in conjugal infidelity' the wicked press, were, as usual, to blame. 'The man who endeavours to obtain the affections of a married woman, is rather applauded, than branded with infamy. The newspapers no longer reprobate the conduct of the frail Fair One, and the Unprincipled Seducer.'

The editor of *The National Magazine* of 5 October 1833, price 1d., took a more light-hearted view of the 'Requisites for a Wife'.

'She is to be lovely in her person and lively in her mind. Her beauty is never to excite particular, only general admiration, and her liveliness never for an instant to approach levity. At the same time she must be no prude, never object to sitting hours tête-à-tête with a man who evidently thinks her handsome, and must take his arm at a ball, assembly or walk, if he offers it.

'She will be clean in her person, and very well dressed, but never long at her toilette. She must not spend money, but be always in fashion. She is to be simple in her diet, yet her table is to be such as to excite the epicures of the day.

'She is to be au fait with every passing event, but not fond of gaiety. She is to know everybody, but not mix much in society. She has to know everything, but not be learned. She is never to be dull, though she must like retirement. She is to be extremely agreeable in society, but without caring for it.

'If she is a mother, her children are to be highly accomplished and dressed with infinite taste, but their governess's wages low, and their clothes cost next to nothing.

'If she be ill or dejected, she is to be highly pleased if her husband takes the opportunity of going from home.'

After generations of carping male editors, the publication of *The Ladies Cabinet* (1832), edited by a mother and daughter, Beatrice and Margaret de Courcy, claiming 'that none but women can speak or write for women' promised greater enlightenment. The *Liverpool Chronicle* hailed the new journal enthusiastically: 'This pretty little magazine especially designed for the use of the British Fair . . . is embellished with four colour pages of the prevailing modes of Female Dress, and contains a choice selection of prose, poetry and new music. It is very neatly got up and sold at the low price of sixpence each number.'

Their promise to 'present our Fair Readers every month an account of the prevailing fashions' brought an anxious riposte from a male reader who insisted on addressing them as 'Sir'.

'Sir. . . . As I believe it is to be part of your interesting publication . . . to consider the Science of Costume, not merely as a subsidiary to female vanity, but likewise to the modesty and chastity of the female mind, I have ventured to send you some observations on the dress of women, which . . . I can trust to your candour to admit. It has been remarked that at periods when morals are most corrupt, the taste of the naked fashion was carried to its greatest excess.'

The information in 'Fashion of the Month' that 'seven or eight breadths of silk are now indispensable for skirts . . . which are lined throughout with stiff muslin' must, presumably, have reassured him. Alternatively, he might have been disconcerted to learn that 'Dresses for grand parties have the corsages cut very low. . . . The sleeves are sometimes puffed into compartments.'

A gossip-type column included such items as:

'The Royal family appear to enjoy the air of Brighton.'

'Notwithstanding reports . . . the Duke of Wellington has not been seriously indisposed. His illness arises from a severe cold during his residence at Walmer.'

'Sir Walter Scott has arrived at Naples, whence it is his intention to return by way of Vienna, and to pay a visit to the illustrious Goethe.'

Editorials dithered between lip-service to the conservative and the progressive. In a feature, 'The Education of Women', the 'ornaments of man's existence' school of thought predominates: '. . . although a lady should not be ignorant of astronomy, I should not wish to see my daughter learned in that or any other branch of science. . . . If a lady has a natural turn for poetry or literary composition I do not see why she should not cultivate it. I should not however, recommend females to enter into the domains of history or philosophy. *When they become grave they are seldom agreeable.* In my opinion an elegant woman is never seen to so much advantage as when she is fully occupied before her workbox with something useful.'

A later article, 'The Decline of Gretna Green', takes a more liberal approach, and even suggests that young women might be allowed 'to think for themselves'.

'Whatever the cause . . . we now hear of few flights of anxious lovers to Gretna

Green. . . . It is now generally admitted that maids of eighteen and twenty may venture to think for themselves upon a matter in which their individual feelings are . . . essentially interested. . . . When they are kept at pickles and preserves, knitting and embroidery, rarely allowed to go to a country ball, it is perhaps neither wonderful nor very blameable if the squire's daughter should sometimes feel disposed to place her fate in the hands of her footman. At the present day, such degradation would be beyond excuse.'

The only escape from 'being kept at pickles and preserves' was that grim fate of becoming a governess. If the qualifications required in 'a letter written by a lady to her brother' in *La Belle Assemblée*, July 1826, may be credited, the only unspecified item was a halo.

'My dear brother. . . . I am in great distress for want of a governess for my daughters. I require a person who is a perfect mistress of music, drawing, dancing, geography, writing, arithmetic and French. She must not only understand French grammatically, but must also . . . speak it correctly and elegantly. A knowledge of Italian would be a great recommendation.

'Of course, she must be a gentlewoman in her manners, well read, well principled, and very good tempered and fond of children, and not objecting to retirement, for we see very little company, and Mr —— and myself like to have our evenings to ourselves. I wish her to be about twenty-five.'

Wryly the brother replies, 'If I should find such a paragon, I would make her not your governess, but my wife.'

Poetry, very properly in an age dedicated to 'sensibility' and 'delicacy', was all but obligatory for women's journals. The pangs of unrequited love, dying flowers, the innocence of children, were its staple themes. Composing it was not without occupational hazards. As *La Belle Assemblée* records:

46

'The well-known Mrs . . . of literary celebrity, met with a serious accident . . . as during a fit of poetical abstraction the candle caught her head-dress, and burnt her hair off so completely that her medical adviser despaired of her ever again recovering that invaluable embellishment.

'However, we are happy to add that a titled friend . . . having experienced the happy effects of Rowland's Oil . . . advised the fair sufferer to try it, and now she has as beautiful a coiffure as nature ever gave to its most favoured daughter.' This was a sneaky example of the 'unsolicited testimonial' ad which, with its snob reference to a 'titled friend', anticipated the women's magazine ads of the 1920s and thirties when peeresses willingly endorsed anything from somebody's cosmetics to someone else's boot polish.

By 1829 *La Belle Assemblée* boasted 'that it was now alone, without rival in the field. . . . Without arrogance or assumption we may say that every feature, every department of our work affords ample evidence of unceasing exertion.' Features included A Monthly Review of New Publications, Music, Drama, and the Fine Arts, Tales of a Physician, The Animal Kingdom, A Country Album, and lists of births, marriages and deaths.

With the weary assumption of superiority peculiar to their calling, the literary critic declared: 'It is not without regret . . . we turn over the insipid pages thrust into our sight at every booksellers. This trash continues to break forth in abundance . . . at a time when the price of paper threatens . . . to put an end to printing.' Worse, it encouraged the working classes to lay claim to emotions reserved exclusively, it seemed, for their betters. 'Sentiments above their station in that part of the nation, who, when they have shut up shop, wet their thumb and spell through a novel. A lovesick chambermaid is enough to ruin half her sisterhood, and high-flown notions of honour set two tailors duelling. . . . There is much to be complained of in other publications . . . those imitators of Sterne whose pages are polluted with ribaldry . . . those compilers of modern tragedy, at which no man wept, unless in pure friendship for the author.'

Ireland provided copy for a popular type of fiction of a patronising genre whose near-imbecilic stock characters spoke a tongue (as George Bernard Shaw later pointed out) unknown to its inhabitants.

'Will ye whist, Judy, a pretty orphin you, Agra, to be imposin' on the gintry. . . . Give me a little sixpence, my Lord, and we'll wish ye a long life and a happy death every day of the year.'

Quaint, quarrelsome or frankly incomprehensible, the 'Orish' could be dismissed. No so those villains across the Channel. Rumour of their 'secret weapon' was allayed for *La Belle Assemblée* readers by their Paris correspondent writing from the rue Saint Dominique, Faubourg St Germain, 20 September 1834.

'Dear Melmouth. . . . You may calm your fears as to the superiority which the French are about to exercise over us in the air, and under the sea. Both experiments have completely failed, and I regret to say the latter has cost the inventor his life. His secret . . . perished with him.

'The failure of the other experiment has been ascribed rather to malice than to accident . . . strong suspicions are entertained that the balloon was purposely damaged. . . . Three-fourths of our *savants* are of opinion that the air is not navigable. I am myself inclined to think so, but when I consider the immense progress that science has made within the last twenty years, my opinion is shaken.

'The theatres are well attended, but the pieces of so licentious a description, that womankind can but seldom attend them.'

Things were ordered differently in England. The 'celebrated Mr Kendel' played Lear at the Haymarket, and Mozart's 'Don Giovanni' made its London debut.

The high standard of articles on architecture, philosophical discussions, and reports on the wars raging across the Continent complete with diagrams of troop dispositions, suggest an intelligent readership curiously at odds with the cretinous fiction. The Gothic continued to flourish with titles reminiscent of the silliest of today's horror films: 'The Sepulchre of the Living', 'The Devil's Barn', 'The Hermit'. A typical passage of dialogue reads:

'Yes, yes, it it is better to part at once', murmured Rosa, as the hot tears fell upon the letter. 'Oh Wilhelm, I had deemed thee not so weak! Where now thy vows, thy promises of eternal fidelity? Yet why these tears? A man who can thus love merely the outer shell and care nothing for the kernel is not worth one sigh! I will conquer this weakness!'

Beauty, so far from being equated with 'Vice' was actually approved by *The Toilet*, a publication of the forties that went so far as to assert: 'That a proper and careful attention to the preservation of personal beauty is not only advisable, but a positive duty in the lady who would exercise her legitimate influence . . . in her domestic circle, or in general society, few will feel disposed to deny.' Disguising your wrinkles was permissible, but 'painting one's face should never be resorted to—it betrays a degraded mind'. And if you were neither beautiful nor degraded—you could always become 'agreeable'. 'What are the talents that contribute to make a female agreeable?' asks *The Ladies Pocket Magazine* (1830). One answer is, dancing. 'It should not, however', youthful readers are cautioned, 'be an art of coquetry . . . but considered a relaxation, an exercise in health.'

To the Abbé Hulot, 'a French fanatic', it was an exercise 'deserving of hell's flames'. As reported in *La Belle Assemblée* (1831) he asks: 'How can one dance, particularly waltz, with a person of a different sex without indulging in the most culpable liberties? In this dance, impurity divested of shame . . . exhibits itself before spectators who are so corrupted as to applaud its excesses. It kills a sense of modesty . . . in those who indulge in it . . . it is a violent poison that carries instantaneous death to the soul . . . rendering them *deserving of hell's flames.*'

Alternatively, music and painting, according to *The Ladies Pocket Museum* were 'useful for persons who have neither understanding nor taste for higher attainments'. Either way, talent was not to be overdone. 'I have seldom known women of genius who were pleasant domestic companions. The piquante originality of such a character is sometimes pleasing in a man, but always ridiculous in a woman. She must know how to bend the mind from the lofty heights of literature or poetry . . . to chit-chat in the drawing room, where one can talk much and say nothing.'

Talking much and saying nothing could include a discussion about the latest hair-styles. 'The hair in its present mode . . . is much elevated on top of the head. Over the forehead are two *bandeaus* of hair, and a bow of three loops on the summit of the hair. A wreath, composed of ears of corn, blue cornflower and scarlet field poppies, with a small wheat-sheaf above the bows of the hair, completes the head-dress.' There was room, too, for criticism of such as 'the vain little creature' seen at a ball, 'whose fingers on the left hand were loaded with diamonds, and who waltzed the greater part of the evening without a glove on that hand'.

Another popular topic among the ladies could arouse conflict between patriotism and inclination: 'Taste in dress is peculiarly a woman's province . . . but let her beware of turning a cold, heedless glance from her own starving countrywomen, her own national manufacturers . . . in order to gratify the vitiated predilection for foreign novelties.'

A blow against these 'vitiated predilections' was struck by no less than Queen Adelaide (wife of William IV, who succeeded George IV in 1830) who intimated that '. . . ladies are to appear at her Court on her birthday in dresses of English manufacture . . . this will essentially serve the interests of commerce.'

Knowing who wore what, was almost as vital as knowing what to wear, and *La Belle Assemblée* devoted pages to the descriptions of illustrious wardrobes. To quote merely two:

'*Countess of Camden*: A dress of beautiful Spanish brown velvet, richly embroidered with gold, and festooned with rich gold ropes and tassels. Head-dress feathers and diamonds.

'*Countess of Bellamont*: A brown velvet dress ornamented with gold shells.'

No 'woman of taste' could, of course, dress without the help of her personal maid. The 'servant problem' was perennial. Commenting on a publication, *The Adventures of a Lady in Search of a Good Servant*, *La Belle Assemblée*'s literary critic observes, 'Its title alone might sell a large edition. That there is "something rotten" in . . . relations between servants and their employers, few among the middle-classes will deny. The lower classes must be better instructed before we can have a race of really good servants . . . happy in the fulfilment of their duties, which, whatever they may think, are seldom as onerous as those of their employers.'

That such problems were not limited to the wealthy, is evidenced by *The Family Economist*, first published in 1848. This penny monthly was 'devoted to the Moral, Physical and Domestic Improvement of the Industrious Classes . . . containing original articles by the Best Writers, on Domestic Economy, Education, Sanitary Reform, Cottage Gardening, Farming, Social Sketches, Moral Tales, Family Secrets and Valuable Household recipes'. The frontispiece of each issue was edged with such precepts as: '*Learn to unlearn what you have learned amiss*', '*Diligence is a fair fortune*', '*Past labour is pleasant delight*'.

In 'A Word to Young Mistresses' it counsels: 'Do not be in a hurry . . . to have a kitchenful of servants. It is not uncommon for a young mistress to hire a young servant with the idea of "bringing her up in her own way". Generally . . . mistress and maid, both inexperienced, blunder on together . . . until the mistress is persuaded to hire a second to help the first, and soon finds a third . . . wanted to help them, and expenses unjustifiably increased.'

Servants' clothes also came under fire, with mistresses urged to 'restrain them from extravagance and inconsistency of dress . . . into which their vanity might lead them. The housemaid and lady's maid, may, with propriety, approach nearer the style of dress of their employer, than the housemaid, laundry-maid or under-servants.'

Up till as recently as the 1920s it was possible to tell at a glance to which station of life a person belonged. Among the articles of dress regarded as unsuitable to the Lower Orders by the *Home Economist* in 1848, 'may be enumerated silk gowns, silk stockings, blond lace, feathers and artificial flowers, bracelets, necklaces, rings and ear-rings'. There were also complaints about servants' hair-styles. 'In the morning they are disfigured with tiers of curl-papers; in the afternoon dressed with long pendant ringlets, to induce which, much time is spent at night when they might be better engaged mending their clothes.'

It was not only improper for servants to dress above their station. It was equally undesirable for them to read above it. 'Never read a book that belongs to your employer without their permission. The education and status of ladies renders some books suitable for them which would be otherwise for a servant. If you read anything that causes you to feel discontented with your station, put it away immediately.'

The *Home Economist* lists the following table, 'consistent with wages of £7 year' considered 'suitable for a servant'.

|  | s. | d. |
|---|---|---|
| 1 good cotton dress | 7 | 8 |
| 2 common working gowns | 7 | 0 |
| Lining for dresses | 2 | 0 |
| 4 petticoats | 8 | 0 |
| Body linen | 4 | 6 |
| Stockings, 3 pairs | 6 | 0 |
| Muslin for caps | | |
| and handkerchiefs | 6 | 0 |
| Bonnets and trimmings | 10 | 6 |
| 4 chequered aprons | | |
| and 2 white ditto | 6 | 0 |
| A shawl | 12 | 0 |
| 3 pairs shoes | 12 | 0 |
| 2 pairs gloves | 1 | 6 |
| Sundries | 10 | 0 |
| Total £4 | 13 | 2 |

# CHAPTER FOUR

# The Dawn of Conscience

'THE year 1839', records *The Ladies Treasury*, 'was a year of much anxiety for the Queen. The spirit of destruction and disloyalty was manifested in the provinces, and in Ireland.' The queen was the youthful Queen Victoria who two years before had slipped almost unobtrusively on to the throne. The report continues: 'The Chartists, armed with pikes, swords, fireballs, hand-grenades and other missiles, proceeded to burn Sheffield, Bradford, Barnsley and other places, including London and Wales. All England was in a more or less unquiet state. In Ireland, with the exception that the Irish did not murder each other, as now, there was a great disloyalty incited by treasonable . . . inflammatory addresses.'

Sentimentalists, given to 'walking backwards to Christmas', tend to invest Victoria's reign (1837–1901) with the aura of a golden age. Britain ruled not only the waves, but vast areas of the globe. 'Wider still and wider shall thy bounds be set' could be sung with conviction. Yet if the queen presided over an Empire 'on which the sun never set', for millions of her subjects it was a quagmire of misery upon which the sun never rose. Elizabeth Fry, Mrs Gaskell, Henry Mayhew and Charles Dickens bore witness to a poverty, human degredation and squalor unknown to our contemporary 'third-rate nation'.

*La Belle Assemblée* outlined the grim fate that awaited the inadequate, the sick, the old, the rebellious, the independent-minded. 'The Poor Houses are cold, white-washed sepulchres. . . . A large proportion of the inmates are women . . . night-wanderers or tramps, orphan children, the lame, blind, idiot and insane, the aged who lie down . . . to die; but by far the worst, the sick outcasts of the streets, thrown up out of the very mire of the gutter.'

Camilla Toumlin, then editing *La Belle Assemblée*, pulled no punches. Comfortably-off readers were discomforted by her injunctions to 'visit some alley or court and see with your own eyes the conditions of our London metropolitan dwelling dens of the poor . . .'

'If every reader . . . would knock at the door of the nearest Union . . . and go home vowing vengeance against a system that tended so to distress the distressed, and degrade the degraded . . . if she would see . . . the old, the sick bedridden women who have lain staring at the whitewashed walls for the last ten years of their lives . . . the wretched, shrivelled children whose food is carried off by the harpies around them . . . surely she would think with us . . . it is high time to awake out of sleep and sound the alarm.

Cosy furs for
the cold days
of January
1847.
(Photograph
by Geoff
Mayor.)

'I am ashamed of you, my idle sisters, for your carelessness and indifference in causing no end of pain, of death and disease.'

If it was a voice crying in the wilderness, it is not without significance that it was raised within the pages of a women's magazine. Nor was it remiss in reminding readers that the rich woman's fashion whim could spell starvation to her sisters as an 1847 issue made clear:

'A poor workwoman writes on behalf of the artificial flower-makers, whose trade, she says, has almost gone out of existence through the use of feathers. If only, she writes, ladies could be induced to wear artificial flowers, it would do us the world of good, as few of us have done more than three or four weeks' work in as many years, the rest have done nothing at all, and hundreds of work people are literally starving.'

Employed women fared scarcely better. *La Belle Assemblée* reminded readers:

'When the woman of fashion surveys herself in the mirror with satisfaction . . . little she dreams of the heartache experienced by the hurried workers . . . dressmakers who have often but twelve hours' notice to begin and finish a dress; the close room, the late retiring and early rising . . . which produces such moral and physical evils.

'No wonder parties of pleasure are preferred to remaining in the dreary back-parlour; no wonder the girl, too frail, too vain, too weak to resist the luxuries offered by her seducer, when contrasted to the twelve, fourteen, and sixteen hours daily labour, succumbs to temptation. . . . At one, two and three o'clock in the morning . . . these girls are frequently seen returning home; their youth and beauty render them objects of attraction to the licentious of the other sex; their extreme poverty inclines them to be easy prey; and the dreadful consequence is that hundreds of them are added to those unfortunates who nightly parade our streets.'

It was an observation underlined by a poem in *The Domestic Magazine* (first published 1804) by the poet Robert Southey.

> I asked her what there was in guilt
> That could her heart allure
> To shame, disease and late remorse;
> She answered, she was poor.

George Bernard Shaw, born nine years later, in 1856, exposed these conditions in his initially banned play, *Mrs Warren's Profession*.

Another cause championed by *La Belle Assemblée*'s campaigning editor, along with the edior of the *Home Economist*, was that of the scandalously overworked 150,000 male and female shop assistants. Both carried reports of meetings held by the metropolitan Early closing Association formed in 1842.

'Previously to the establishment of the Society, the hours of employment . . . were excessive; it was common practice for the linen drapers to keep their shops open . . . till eleven and twelve o'clock at night, it being often 1 a.m. and sometimes two o'clock in the morning before assistants were free. On Sundays they were not infrequently put to work until three, four and five o'clock. . . . It is a common cry to say "if we give our shopmen more leisure they will only abuse it . . . spending their time and money in vicious indulgences".'

'So long as the public will buy at unseemly hours' Mr Wakely M.P. told them, 'shops will be kept open . . . and the youth of Great Britain suffer a slavery scarcely exceeded by any under the skies of heaven.'

Camilla Toumlin echoed his sentiments. 'Woe to those who supinely sit in content, soothing their easy consciences with the cuckoo-note, 'exaggeration', while thousands of helpless children pine away their lives in labour and destitution more severe than any ever produced by negro slavery.'

Frontispiece of *The English Woman's Domestic Magazine*, 1856. Author's collection. (Photograph by Geoff Mayor.)

Factual reporting drove the message home. 'The life-expectancy of an artisan is twenty-two years. Among the higher classes, forty-four.'

'In the calamatious season just past, manufacturers have been at a standstill. Food has been unobtainable by the poor, for employment they had none. Offspring have . . . pined and wasted away. In the dense, crowded rooms where the poor hive together, contagious disease makes rapid progress.

'In Liverpool, 13,546 deaths were recorded between January and September 1847 from cholera and fever.'

'The number of children who die in infancy in English towns, average 385 out of every 1,000.'

'The cholera in London has carried off upwards of 10,000 persons . . . a loss equal to the Battle of Waterloo once a month.'

These were distasteful facts, skimmed over indifferently perhaps by readers more concerned with the still Paris-dominated fashions. Without French, a woman could scarcely have ordered her wardrobe. *Mantles* were trimmed with *sable camils*. *Capotes douilettes* became fashionable. Winter styles included *passementerie*. *Sautache* was again popular. The *paletot* was in *vogue*. Black was favourite for *pardessus*. The *toilette* must be rendered *le dernier gout*. Muslin undersleeves terminated in a single *bouillon*. All of which was enough to have given True Englishman a heart attack. Yet contrary to what may be supposed, it owed nothing to the pretentiousness that transforms today's shops into *boutiques*, and Dick and Charlie, hairdressers, into Ricardo and Carlos, *coiffuriers*, but resulted from the influx of French émigrés who, along with their dressmakers, milliners and hairdressers, sought refuge in England from the snap-happy guillotine.

London as always acted as a magnet. In vain the *Domestic Journal* warned:

'If the advice of one who knows . . . might be offered to any stranger intending to settle in the metropolis, it is "keep away". Wages are low, hours long, work spasmodic. Half-starve in the country rather than wholly starve in London. The workhouses are full, the prisons are full, the streets are full, the workshops are full. Keep away.'

Half-starving in the country involved women and children labouring fifteen to sixteen hours a day in cotton-mills, coal-mines, on farms. But not everyone went hungry in the Hungry Forties. As *La Belle Assemblée* records, 'At a recent ball, Queen Margaret of Italy wore a Court dress of gold brocade, an extraordinary quantity of diamond ornaments, and a diamond tiara, and around her neck twelve rows of magnificent pearls.'

Such glaring social inequalities may have inspired Benjamin Disraeli's novel, *Sybille, a story of Two Nations*, enthusiastically reviewed in this magazine in 1845. 'The two nations are the rich and the poor. The cry of the suffering is heard at last . . . the rich bend down their ears to listen to it, and to . . . open their eyes to scenes long sealed up, within factory walls, or in loathesome, thronging mines.'

The same year saw their publication of the obituary of that great champion of the poor, Thomas Hood. 'What a sad picture . . . do the last months of this great man's

## PERAMBULATORS.

VISITORS to London and one or two of our largest towns must have seen an improvement which has taken place during the last few months in that small, but not unimportant class of vehicles, children's carriages.

Instead of being dragged along the causeway in no very dignified fashion, the little dears are now propelled from behind, the position of both propeller and propelled being changed considerably for the better. Formerly, a lady, or the semblance of one, would not willingly be seen performing the office of beast of burden in a public thoroughfare; nor was it always safe to trust this duty to a young nurse, the carriage behind being exposed to sundry mishaps, besides occasional attacks from mischievous boys. The ease, safety and comparative pleasantness and respectability of the whole affair with the improved carriages — perambulators they are called—is seen at a glance. Many a mother may now be seen taking a pleasant walk, with the little one securely placed under her eye, and propelled by a very slight effort. The price of these pretty and useful little vehicles at Burton's establishment, 487, New Oxford Street, is from two to three guineas for "Iron Perambulators lined with chintz for the Million." With additional seats, and more expensive linings, &c. the prices rise to six guineas. An illustrated circular has been sent to us, on application, from the above place, containing a number of designs for children's and invalids' carriages; also trucks for commercial purposes, all of the new construction, which for appearance, and, we should think, use and convenience, will suit the taste and purposes of most persons who require them.

life display. The "Song of the Shirt" was knocking at the breast of every heart in Great Britain, while its author, propped up in bed, panting for breath, was trying to enlist . . . his friends to launch the magazine that still bears his name. Latterly his friends had been agonised by his terrible lament—"I cannot die . . .". Such friends were grateful to lay him on 10th May in a calm grave at Kensal Green.'

Unlike those other 'exposers of things long sealed up', Mrs Gaskell and Charles Dickens, Hood died poverty-stricken. In 1850, Dickens published *Household Words*, a 2d. weekly, which ran for eight years. Between novel-writing, editing, public readings and extensive travelling, this apparently tireless author was also interested in amateur dramatics. *La Belle Assemblée* reports how, together with illustrators Cruikshank, Mark Lemon, Frank Stone and Augustus Egg, he appeared in a benefit performance, staged in Liverpool, in aid of the aged, impoverished poet, Leigh Hunt.

'Had Charles Dickens tried acting as a profession, he would unquestionably have become as popular in that, as he is in his present distinguished position', wrote the theatre critic.

The train that took them all to Liverpool was supplied free by the railway company. Inevitably, 'the railway age' accelerated the pace of life. Yet contrary to ourselves, the Victorians saw science not as a potential threat, but as a 'happy advance'. To quote again from *La Belle Assemblée*:

'In our grandfathers' days everything went slowly. It was a journey of many days from London to York, and one never undertaken except under pressure of . . . imperative business, or by the very wealthy. What stories are told of will-making, or robbery by highway robbers, before starting on an expedition of even a hundred miles, so fraught with danger was it supposed to be.

'As for the post, it was tedious and expensive. . . . In those days business must have been managed in a more leisurely manner . . . than at present, when rapid communication both personally, and by letter, goes far to make every occupation a stirring and busy one. No one with common sense can refuse to see that in the last quarter of a century, a great and happy advance has been made.'

Hints on 'reading on railways' were offered to 'the inexperienced traveller' by the *Home Economist*. 'To read when in a railway train, hold a card . . . across the book over the line below that which you are reading. The eye is then relieved from the disturbance caused by the motion of the carriage.' Advertisements offered additional comfort for the traveller in the form of travelling rugs and foot-warmers.

Not merely individual travellers but whole populations were on the move. Ireland, gripped by the potato famine, saw vast numbers of her population emigrate to the New World. Berlin, Vienna, Rome, Milan, Naples, Prague and Budapest, as *La Belle Assemblée* reported, were scenes of riots, mayhem, social injustice, unrest. In Britain, desperation, starvation and unemployment, as much as the self-righteously condemned 'lust for gold', drove families by their thousands to join in the Californian Gold Rush of 1848, or to seek new lives in Australia. While *La Belle Assemblée*'s delicate heroine, Grace Clifford, 'reclined on a sofa . . . her eyes half-closed, with a face as pale as the white rose in her bosom', planning her new ball gown, women at the other end of the social ladder coped with undreamed-of hardships.

'The number of people who left the kingdom in the year 1852 was at the rate of one thousand a day. Let anyone imagine what would be the effect produced by a thousand people a day pouring into some town in England of 30,000 inhabitants, and a faint idea may be formed of the state of things in Melbourne. Those who arrive unprovided with a tent find themselves in a miserable condition, for it is utterly impossible to get lodgings.

'. . . the immigrants, weary of their long journey, eager to set foot in the new country, are made to pay 8s. each passage from the vessel to the town, where they are landed . . . often in pouring rain, or scorching heat, or in a fierce dust-storm. They find that not a place of shelter is to hand, and all the necessities of life are at a frightful price, and that impudence and insolence hold sway.

'Then there is the voyage out, lasting from eighty to one hundred and twenty days
. . . the whole period is one of unmitigated misery . . . Ship-owners know that once
at sea they can laugh at passengers' complaints. When complaining about stinking

water served out . . . on a voyage to New York, the mate told us "if we didn't like it, we might get out and walk".'

Practical as well as cautionary advice was offered to would-be immigrants by the *Family Economist*. Men bound for Australia were told to take 'clothes of strong fustian or leather and thick woollen undershirts'. Men and women needed waterproof cloaks, six shirts or skirts, six pairs of stockings and two pairs of shoes each. Required domestic equipment included: a mattress, bolster, blankets, sheets, towels, kettles, saucepans, fire-irons, smoothing-irons, candlesticks. 'Those bound for the diggings will need a pick-axe, draining-spade, light steel fork, a shovel, crowbar, iron wedges, a sledge-hammer, tin platters, and a cradle for washing the clay and gravel.'

Not all the sharks were in the sea. Readers were warned against tricksters disappearing with their cash, advised to inspect ships before buying their tickets (at anything from £15 to £70 a time) and to insist upon written contracts for their passage. And they were warned: 'None should go but those who can bear hardship . . . in the hope of future comfort. Otherwise they will lament the day they ever left England.'

Reports home from some of the '150,000 who sailed to Australia since May' were scarcely encouraging.

'Among a few nice things to be had gratis in this "beautiful colony",' reads a letter, 'I may mention snakes five feet long . . . dragon-flies by the million . . . native cats very destructive of poultry . . . fleas . . . rats—we killed thirty a fortnight ago.

'It is impossible to keep oneself clean, what with the sand and the hot winds . . . one dreadfully hot . . . the other cold enough for a great-coat . . . and such rain as I never saw in England. As to the wind . . . it is no uncommon thing for roofs to blow off, and all wooden houses dance and shake. . . . Dysentry is very prevalent.'

Not all hopes were dashed. As the *Home Economist* notes (1854), 'In the Brewhouse Ragged School magazine (Wapping), for October 1850, it was stated that Patrick Maloney . . . assisted under the auspices . . . for Ragged School emigrants' wrote to his benefactors, 'This is to inform you I have been to the gold diggings and have been a little successful, and I am now sending my mother a little money.' The 'little money'—fifty pounds—was a considerable sum in those days. It was, as the editor commented 'an instance where the liberality of those who found a free passage for a destitute boy to Australia, was not misplaced'.

# CHAPTER FIVE

# *Fact and Fiction*

THE year 1844 saw the introduction into Britain of the Christmas card, and the polka. Mr J. Mallord William Turner exhibited his *Wind, Rain and Steam* at the Royal Academy. The column erected to Nelson's memory five years before in Trafalgar Square was already a familiar landmark. So too were the new Houses of Parliament designed by Sir James Barry. *La Belle Assemblée* noted another innovation. 'A novelty with which not many will be familiar is the adoption by a few families in England of that pretty German custom, the Christmas tree.'

If 'sensibility' was the theme of former fiction, sentimentality marked the latter period of the age. *La Belle Assemblée*'s 'heroines' were, to a woman, 'inspired by lofty sentiments', invested with a 'bloom' which 'once lost could never be called back'. 'Countenances' were unfailingly 'divine', 'beautiful', 'fair'. Ringlets were always 'glossy', eyes 'bright' and/or 'dilated with exalted aspirations', 'filled with lustre', 'glowing with love'. Brows were 'pure and unclouded'.

'At seventeen she was really divine . . . before the rough finger of the world had brushed from the just-ripening fruit that delicate bloom that can never be called back.'

'Drawing up her sylph-like figure . . . and shaking back her glossy ringlets from her beautiful face, she turned away with a smile of haughty derision.'

'Her eyes dilated with exalted aspiration, and her brow was calm with the pure reflections of an innocent mind.'

Alas, neither 'bloom' nor 'exalted aspirations' were proof against 'the rough finger of the world' for these saccharine creations. Not at least for the first fifteen chapters. In Jane Austen's *Pride and Prejudice* Mr Bennett observes, 'Next to being married, a girl likes to be crossed in love a little, now and then.' And few girls could have been 'crossed', crushed, rejected or renounced more effectively than those enclosed within *La Belle Assemblée*'s covers. Spurned by top-drawer heroes with names like Cholmondeley, Wainwright, Cavendish, Maitland, Fitzroy, they 'fade away', 'die of broken hearts', 'decline into early graves'. Heads 'sink down on bosoms'. Cold hands 'clasp in despair'. Eyes 'grow dim'. Noble sentiments abound.

'Let him be happy, if he forget me and love another!'

'Alas, alas for women's love! How often is her deep devotion repaid by bitter, cutting insult, cold, cruel, heartless scorn! Poor, poor Laura! Heavy, heavy was her trial, bitter, bitter, her misery.'

'We see her in pure innocence . . . beneath the influence of first love. . . . Again behold her, pale, spirit-broken, her bright hopes crushed, fading away, sinking into an early grave.'

'In dread of vexing him who had wrung her with sorrow, that pure, that loving creature crushed down her every feeling with . . . cheeks unmoistened by a single tear.'
Elsewhere 'tears course down pale cheeks' at the slip of an antimacassar.

'Her eyes grew strangely dim. Another moment and her tears broke forth . . .'

'Mabel's tears fell thick and fast. She wept, and murmured not.'

'Oh father!' she cried, 'I loved him!' But as she spoke the tears burst forth again, and she flung herself sobbing on my breast.'

'Sophia sat, her harp before her, but . . . the melancholy remembrance of . . . Wainwright, brought tears coursing down her pale cheeks.'

'Sterling saw the tears gathering in Edwina's eyes'—and seconds later he too, was hard at it: '. . . a deep groan burst from his lips, and tears started between his hands, fast clasped over his face.'

' "Oh my poor boy! Your guilty, miserable, father!" And could Frank have heard the sobs that followed, his heart must surely have relented.'
Heroines and heroes alike were 'gnawed', 'wormed', tormented' by 'dark secrets', 'pitiless remorse'.
'Clara turned as white as marble. It was a comfort to have someone to whom she could disclose the terrible secret which pressed heavily upon her breaking heart.'

' "Mother!" cried the girl, "Do you not know me? I am Elaine, your child!" "No, no!" exclaimed Martha wildly. "It is my *own child* I want, my bright-eyed Hester!" Then all was still. She was dead, and her secret with her.'
Heroines who survived to the last chapter received the full hearts and flowers treatment.
' "Rosaline, will you not reply?" he implored. "What can I say, Walter? Your declaration is so sudden, so unexpected!" "Unexpected? Rosaline, you must have known I loved you! That you were the day-star of my life, my fountain of inspiration, dearest!" '
A different type of heroine appeared with the publication of Charlotte Brönte's

*Jane Eyre* (1847). Published under the name Currer Bell, 'this first work of a new young author' was praised by *La Belle Assemblée*'s critic for its 'manly style. Mr Bell has produced a heroine unlike the general class of novel-heroine . . . one with no claim to personal beauty.' By contrast, her hero became the stock perennial of all women's magazines. Mr Rochester, sardonic, attractive, fortyish, still stalks the pages of the romantic weeklies. Yet Charlotte's creep-mouse heroine and idealised hero pale into insignificance beside the flesh and blood, love-hate relationship of Heathcliff and Cathy in Emily Brontë's *Wuthering Heights*, published the same year. Heathcliff, savage and uncouth, forerunner of the anti-hero, is still too meaty for under hair-dryer consumption.

Cathy, for all her rompings on the moor, did not commit, or produce the 'fruits' of committing, 'that most heinous of crimes' with its 'consequences of frenzies of unhallowed passion'. No so Lucy, the 'innocent country girl' whose 'bloom' caught the lecherous eye of the wicked squire. Yet *La Belle Assemblée*'s story assessment of the fate of the unmarried mother, was as much fact as fiction: 'Lucy Merton had swelled the ranks of the roué's victims. Lucy was a mother. The finger of scorn was pointed at her. Old companions shunned her. The world closed its gates upon her, for to the fallen there is no return; every face is averted; every respectable employment closed to her; she must sink lower and lower into the quagmire of sin.'

Girls who got their man to the altar had thenceforth to propitiate him like some tribal god as was made clear in 'Home Truths for Home Peace', 1855: 'Far beyond the drawing room is the consecration of one room to the special use of the Master of the House. A sound and lovely policy that secures a husband. . . . Should business or amusement induce a temporary absence, the image of his *own* room, and the gentle, loving being presiding over its many indulgences . . . will guide him safe back again.'

Yet even 'man's freedom to look about him, to choose, to marry at his leisure' could be more apparent than real. Unlike today's seemingly orphaned heroines and heroes, nineteenth-century fiction reflects the prevailing, often tyrannical, parental domination. Tradition, religion, convention, economics established the Master of the House as an entrenched hearth-rug Hitler, a Fireside Führer. And in an age when the weakest went to the wall it is not difficult to appreciate that the claims of romantic love weighed little against the threat of lifelong poverty to a daughter or son. Not that the participants saw it that way.

' "I do not blame you, Henry," said Constance, as the tears fell fast from her eyes. "Your father could not have forced you to love another. . . . Farewell! I wish you happiness, though you have blighted mine forever!" '

' "Oh Frank, no!" cried Minnie, pushing back her long hair which was wet with tears. "Precious as your love is, I will not come between you and a parent." '

In *Pride and Prejudice* Jane Austen derides Mrs Bennett's anxious, 'What's to become of our girls?' The wealthy apart, it was no laughing matter. But Mrs Bennett's mindless chatter is no match for the loquacity of *La Belle Assemblée*'s fictional mamas. To a woman they can hold forth for minutes on end without drawing breath.

'Mrs Churchill hemmed down a sigh. "I will not stop now", she said, "to tell you whether I think you impatient or not, but will rather go on to explain why I felt impelled this evening to urge you, and why, although you will not allow me to lift the curtain, I have been unable to refrain from making some effort to give a happier turn to your thoughts, evidently of late somewhat burdensome to you." ' The monologue continues for pages of close type. When the long-suffering son manages to get a word in edgeways, the author interposes 'here the entrance of the tea-tray broke off the conversation'—not surprisingly, since it apparently arrives without human aid.

Papas, given to ejaculations like 'Pshaw!' were equally verbose. In *Florence, A tale of Women's Friendship* by best-selling author Grace Aquilar, Lord Glenvylle, one of the 'dark secret' school, who 'for shameful reasons of his own' opposes his son's marriage, prefaces his 'confession' with a hundred-word, non-stop preamble.

Such indulgences were limited to the wealthy. The poor were otherwise preoccupied. There was, for instance, the ever-recurring cholera. To quote *The Family Economist*, 1853: 'At the time this article is penned, the cholera is once more established in Britain. Need we tell readers that these foster-houses of cholera were

## EIGHTEEN-PENNY WASHING MACHINE.

AT most American warehouses may be seen a simple contrivance for saving the knuckles of the washerwoman, which is nothing more than a board about eighteen inches by fourteen, with the surface cut into smooth ribs on one side. The board is held in a slanting direction in the left hand, the lower portion being in the wash-tub and the ribs extending cross-ways. The clothes are soaked in the usual manner, and then commences the rubbing upwards and downwards across the ribs of the board. It is said to answer well. The same plan is adopted in Germany and other parts of the Continent, and the good wives, both there and in America, marvel that English washerwomen continue to wear off their knuckles, when they might save them at so trifling an expense as eighteen-pence, which is all this article costs.

the filthy, undrained, unventilated, over-crowded districts and houses in town and village . . . those are the places in which fever and like diseases find a congenial soil.'

Just as the Elizabethans relied upon blood-letting, the Georgians upon the efficacy of drinking sea and/or Spa water (and we fly to tranquillisers), so the Victorians pinned their faith on 'flannel next to the skin'. The *Home Economist* advised: 'If your constitution is delicate, wear flannel next to the skin. . . . We have heard an eminent physician say that a large proportion of deaths from cholera . . . would have been prevented by this simple precaution.'

As always there was no shortage of advice about what women ought to do or be. 'Women ought to measure from 27 inches round the waist . . . but thousands are laced down to less than twenty inches by means of wood, whalebone and steel, and the chest often reduced to half its proper size.'

Tight lacing, it was warned, could lead to—red noses: 'If a foolish girl by dint of squeezing with busk and bones, secures . . . a wasp-waist, she is tolerably certain to gain . . . a red nose. .∴. Surely the most perverse admirer of a distorted spine and compressed lungs, would deem the acquisition of a dram-drinker's nose too heavy a condition to be complied with?'

Editors, as ever, pursued their will o' the wisp dreams of feminine perfection. This time it was 'The Prompt girl': 'The prompt girl rises with the lark. . . . She springs from her bed and in a few minutes is dressed . . . to assist her mother. She never keeps the table waiting. She is never late for prayers. She is never late for school, never late for church. She saves all the time a dilatory girl spends . . . in reading frivolous matter, and gazing idly into vacancy.'

More recognisable is 'The Model Daughter' as described in the *Home Economist*, borrowing from *Punch*: 'She comes down to breakfast before the tea-things are taken away. She curls her own hair, and can undress herself without a maid. She is happy . . . without going to a ball every night. She does not have her letters addressed to the pastry-cook's, or make a postman of the housemaid. . . . She does not read novels in bed. . . . She is not perpetually embroidering mysterious braces . . . or having a Turkish slipper on hand for a mysterious foot in the Guards. She does not keep her mother waiting an hour at a party 'for just another waltz'. She does not take long walks . . . and come home saying she has lost her way.'

Humour (*Home Economist* again borrowing from *Punch* 1849) illustrates themes both contemporary and eternal . . .

*Fallacies of the Gentlemen*

That dinner is to be ready for them the very minute they come into the house.

That a lady's bonnet can be put on as quickly as a gentleman's hat.

That we can dress in a minute; and that ringing the bell violently has the effect of making us dress one bit the quicker.

That they can do everything better than we can, from nursing the baby to poking the fire.

That it is necessary to make a poor woman cry because a shirt button comes off.

That we are not allowed to faint or have the smallest fit of hysterics without being told not to make fools of ourselves.

That housekeeping does not require any money, and if we venture to ask for it, that it is pleasant to be met with . . . black looks, and insinuations as to what we can do with it all; or very agreeable to be told that we will be the ruin of him, some day.

That houses never require cleaning, or tables rubbing; or carpets, beating; or the furniture renewing, or the sofas fresh covers, or in fact that anything has the right to wear out, or to be spilt or broken, and in short, everything has to last for ever.

That a poor lone woman is never to have any pleasure, but to stay at home and mind the children.

That no husband is perfect, like Hercules, without his club; that the less a wife sees of her husband, the fonder she grows of him.

*Fallacies of the Ladies*

That a tight corset is the main-stay of beauty.

That a husband has a peculiar pleasure in stopping to look at every shop he passes when his wife takes him out for a walk.

That thin shoes are conducive to health.

That anything is good so long as it is bought as a bargain.

That no journey is properly carried out excepting with an immense quantity of luggage.

That it is necessary to defer the meaning of a letter until the postscript.

That a young lady loses position if she is in the habit of going down into the kitchen.

That it is proof of gentility to affect not to know what there is for dinner.

That hysterics are the best argument for bringing a person round to the lady's way of thinking.

That no well-bred mother ought to put foot in the nursery.

Nurseries, needless to say, were the prerogative of the well-to-do. Similarly 'romance' for the middle and upper classes became 'mere animal passion' when indulged by the poor. 'Family life' among people of little or no education was a 'multitude of sickly children'. The lamentable state of general education is revealed by contemporary marriage registers. 'In 1846 there were 47,488 men and 70,145 women who signed the register with marks. In England . . . out of those who marry, two out of three men, and one out of every two women are unable to write.' (*Home Economist*, 1849.)

Other complaints have an ominously familiar ring. 'There has, during the last few months, been an enormous advance on the cost of almost all necessities of life. We pay eleven pence for a loaf which last spring cost only sixpence. A joint of meat for which we are charged eighteen pence a pound would, some time since, have been sixpence. Bacon and cheese have experienced a rapid rise from 25% to 50% in prices. Butter too, is dearer. Raisins and currants are more than double the price two years since.'

'Any advance received in wages . . . is not commensurate with the cost of the necessities of life . . . Thirty shillings is now required to purchase the same amount . . . that a year ago would be obtained with twenty.'

Reaction was inevitable. 'At Stockport a number of spinners have come out on strike, and express their determination to remain so, until their terms are agreed.'

'There are more causes than one to account for the present scarcity and dearness of coals. In consequence of the increased demand . . . wages have risen . . . the men earning in two or three days sufficient to purchase the necessities of life . . . get drunk during the remainder of the week. How degraded must be the habits of those people . . . unable to resist resorting to the ale house, and spending half their time in idleness. . . . No doubt the folly of the miners has added several shillings per ton to the price of coals.'

'According to the Factory Commissioners report, an operative works in England, sixty-nine hours for eleven shillings a week.'

Sunday trading was a much-disputed topic. The *Home Economist* reported: 'A mob of 100,000 Londoners assembled on three successive Sundays in Hyde Park . . . in opposing the measure against Sunday trading. "The mob is right", says the *Sunday Times*, "the people will come armed next time." '

Other Londoners flocked to the theatres to see 'Rachel, the dark-browed Queen of Tragedy', as Camille; and Jenny Lind the singer 'irresistibly attractive still. Every night the house is filled to excess.' (*La Belle Assemblée*, 1847.)

*La Belle Assemblée*'s literary critic was less kind to 'the great lexicographer' Dr Johnson, whose alleged 'feebleness of heart and narrowness of mind' made him—in his view, repellent. Nor was the 'great lexicographer's' maxim, 'Patriotism is the last refuge of a scoundrel' in accord with the times. In 1854 the Russians decided to 'defend Christianity and the Holy Places'—to 'protect Greek Christians in Turkey'. The British, French and Turks saw in such noble motives only 'the rising tide of Russian Imperialism'. The result was the Crimean war.

'England is at war', wrote the editor of the *Home Economist* (1854). 'The fact is a startling one to millions who, having been born since the Battle of Waterloo find it difficult to believe that the peace under which we have flourished for nearly half a century, could ever be disturbed again. . . . If we do not draw the sword . . . in a few years, the great, barbaric power of Russia will have swollen to such a pitch, that she will seize England and make it a little province of her over-grown dominions.'

The subsequent defeats and set-backs could always, in some inexplicable fashion, be blamed not on politicians or the Army, but on 'the nation'. 'Our disasters' according to the Englishwoman's Domestic Magazine (edited by S. O. Beeton) 'bring to recollection the over-confident manner in which we commenced the war. We add to our wrong by ascribing our ill-success to mismanagement. The entire nation is at fault.'

A dispatch from the battle-front revealed: 'The siege of Sebastopol continues. One of the wonders of the age is the electric telegraph . . . now completed between London and the Crimea, by which Intelligence is conveyed four thousand miles in a few hours.'

A more significant 'wonder of the age' was a brisk, thirty-year-old young woman named Florence Nightingale. Until then, a 'nurse' was typified by Dickens's Mrs Gamp, a harpy whose grubby hands more readily embraced the gin-bottle than soothed a fevered brow. At the time of the Crimea, Florence Nightingale, defying her upper-class background, had studied nursing in England and abroad. A letter in *The Times* deploring the conditions in the Crimean 'hospitals' inspired her to offer her services, and those of thirty-seven like-minded nurses, to the War Office. Reluctantly, and mainly owing to her influential connections, they were accepted.

The *Home Economist* reports: 'An inferno of misery awaited them at Scutari . . . soldiers lay dying in blood, urine, gangrene, amputations had to be performed in full sight of the patients . . . the stench from the hospital could be smelled outside the walls.' Overcoming ministerial and military bone-headedness, Florence Nightingale reduced the mortality rate from 42 to 2 per cent in mere months.

'Miss Nightingale', records *The Englishwoman's Domestic Journal* (Vol. 8, 1860), 'heroine of the horrible Scutari hospital, has written a little book *Notes on Nursing*. Her remarks on ventilation, fresh air, cleanliness, pure water and drainage, show alike the reflective mind and practised hand.'

This somewhat patronising write-up was the work of another woman whose name was destined to become a household word, Mrs Beeton of cook-book fame. *The Englishwoman's Domestic Journal* was first published by her husband Mr S. O. Beeton in 1852. Its illustrators included John Constable R.A. and William Turner. Between 1852 and 1856 its circulation rocketted from 5,000 to 50,000 a month. Isabella Beeton never lived to become the buxom bossy woman conjured up by her name. Her cookery book with its 'tried and tested recipes' was started when she was twenty-three, finished when she was twenty-seven. Two years later she died.

At the age of twenty-two, Samuel Orchart Beeton (1831–77) had leapt to fame as the British publisher of Mrs Harriett Beecher Stowe's best-selling *Uncle Tom's Cabin*. Other publications followed, including *The Young Englishwoman* (amalgamating with *La Belle Assemblée*) and *The Queen*, still flourishing as *The Queen and Harper's Bazaar*. His flair for spotting winners led to the serialisation of Nathanial Hawthorne's *Scarlet Letter* (*Domestic Journal*) and Louisa Allcott's *Little Women* (*Young Englishwoman*). He was the originator of Christmas Annuals, dictionaries of information, and biographies in weekly or monthly parts, and the first publisher to anticipate the new markets for women's magazines, following the Compulsory Education Act of 1870.

Mingled with Mrs Beeton's recipes, were 'hints on how to destroy bedbugs' and 'how to nurse the now prevalent typhoid fever'. Typical articles were 'The Royal families of Europe', 'Among the Americans' and 'Curious Weddings and Remarkable Marriages'.

Periodically deserting the kitchen range, Mrs Beeton reappeared as fashion writer. Thanks to Queen Victoria's patronage, Ramsgate was now *the* resort. From its wind-swept esplanades Mrs Beeton reported: 'There is something especially picturesque in the appearance of the ladies who now crowd seaside place. The soft muslin, the floating scarf, the coquettish hat with its drooping feather, make the presence of the ladies pictorial to the highest degree.'

The 'attractions' of Ramsgate appeared in a different light to the author of some verse published in *La Belle Assemblée* in 1847:


THE SANDS AT RAMSGATE

by Mrs Adby (abridged)

I traced on my tablets a brace of love-sonnets
Then strolled to the beach and the concourse surveyed
Of beaux in buff slippers, and belles in straw bonnets,
And children, each armed with a bucket and spade.
I paused, I beheld my loved-one advancing,
She held Disraeli's last work in her hands;
I hastened to greet her, my heart began dancing,
And I fondly resolved to make love on the sands.

'Oh lady,' I cried, 'this calm ocean announces
The empire of Summer, soft, pure and serene.'
But she could not reply, for her crisp muslin flounces
Were caught in the wheels of a clumsy machine.
'To me' I resumed, 'thou art dearer than any;
And though little I boast of wealth, houses or lands,
Yet love—' but the outcry of 'Chairs for a penny'
Disturbed the 'smooth course' of my love on the sands.

I poured forth some tender poetic quotations,
When a donkey beside me discordantly brayed!
I vowed to be true through life's toils and temptations,
When I heard a voice ask 'Would I please to be weighed?'

I railed at the world, but my fair one was bending
With infinite grace to a simpering friend;
I heaved a deep sign, but she was attending
To a cryer announcing 'A boat to Ostend.'

My speech about love's first delicious emotion
Was spoiled by the clamour of 'Seed cakes for lunch'
My promise of deep and unchanging devotion
Was drowned by the wrangles of Judy and Punch!

Ye lovers who long to disclose your affection
And feel undecided how best you may woo,
Make love if you please, at a county election,
A Concert at Jullien's, a Hyde Park Review,
A race when loud shouts are proclaiming the winner,
The Custom House stairs when a steam-vessel lands,
An auction, a ship launch, a Mansion House dinner,
But don't go to Ramsgate, to court on the sands!

Bath, Cheltenham, Harrogate and Leamington Spa still held their own as fashion-resorts. Leamington Spa was for a time the home of best-selling author, Nathanial Hawthorne, whose *Scarlet Letter* was serialised in the *Domestic Magazine* of 1858. The degradation of the infamous letter 'A' for adultery, attached to the woman involved, extended likewise to the 'fruit of her guilty passion'.

'Day after day she looked fearfully into the child's expanding nature . . . dreading to detect some dark peculiarity that should correspond with the guiltiness to which she owed her being.'

Under the terms of the new Divorce Bill (1858) a wife's adultery, readers were told, was sufficient grounds for her husband to get a divorce. For a wife however, 'simple adultery was not enough. She must be prepared to prove adultery, cruelty and desertion . . . but it does not follow that a divorce will ensue.'

London and its continued growth caused gloomy forebodings. 'If the population continues to increase as it did between 1841–51, before the end of the century it will contain six million souls. . . . Men are at a loss to picture the possible economy of six million . . . human beings living in one city.'

The 'new electric light' which illuminated Westminster Bridge was poor comfort to those living 'in the backstreets of our great city . . . the overland route of every form of epidemic disease' and the editors of *La Belle Assemblée*, the *Home Economist* and the *Ladies Domestic Magazine* were at one in campaigning for the better conditions urged by the Sanitary Movement.

Another innovation likely to be seen only in more prosperous areas was 'that small but not unimportant class of vehicle, children's carriages, called Perambulators. Instead of being dragged along the causeway . . . the little dears are

now propelled from behind.' Iron perambulators lined with chintz cost from three
to six guineas—the equivalent of a year's wages for a large proportion of workers.
Among those 'lucky' enough to find work, readers were reminded, were seam-
stresses 'sewing from nine in the morning till nine at night for six shilling a week
. . . mantle-makers, straw-hands and flower-makers who get six shillings a week
for twelve hours labour a day.'

'No wonder', the *Domestic Magazine* quotes Prison Inspector F. Hill as saying, 'the
labour of these females . . . requires a greater power of endurance and self control
than can reasonably be expected.'

Women's prisons, such as Holloway, Tothill Fields, Wandsworth, Pentonville,
Millbank and Brixton (not to mention the notorious prison-hulks transporting their
cargoes of human misery to Australia), readers were told, were 'overcrowded'.

In the course of a lengthy article bent on stirring the consciences of their middle-class readership, the *Ladies Domestic Magazine* stated: 'We believe there is not a more heart-rending scene ... than that of the large workshops in our metropolitan prisons, where clad in ... sad-coloured dress, and surrounded by a silence as complete as the tomb, a vast mass of female infamy is spread before the beholder. Out of 23,392 females ... a large number are found to be suffering from ... starvation, intoxication and dissipation. Those in for longer sentences are chiefly child murderers.'

'Visiting a Madhouse' was another assignment from which a contemporary women's magazine—*The Ladies Magazine*, did not shrink.

'All the aggravations that irresponsible tyranny, malice, inhuman torture, and the exercise of every species of cruelty could inflict on the happless sufferer, was practised ... while the unrestrained passions of their brutal keepers was let loose on these miserable creatures.

'A thick litter of straw covers the floor and forms the bed of the wretched inmates. A strong belt round the loins attaches the victim by a chain to a staple in the wall. All are naked.' That some degree of improvement was achieved, was due, as the *Ladies Magazine* recounts, to Miss Dix, an American school-teacher who 'by the force of her conviction elicited a promise of a Parliamentary enquiry'.

While some women were being driven to madness and/or prison by privation, other women were being almost equally frustrated by boredom. 'If', wrote the editor of *The Young Englishwoman*, 'women in the upper or middle ranks of life fritter away their time on worsted works, wax flowers and potichomaine, we are not aware that anyone demands it of them. We do not believe they are ... expected to be merely well-dressed dolls ... and cry ... "I am a-weary, weary in this dreary do-nothingness." ' The remedy was 'to go into your father's study and select ... books on history, biography, logic, law, theology and metaphysics ... and read nothing else until you have thoroughly mastered the subject. You cannot imagine how refreshing the proceeding will be. But if', the writer adds, 'you have not sufficient brains for this, take a saw and plane and hammer and manufacture a chair, table or box.'

More fortunate lower-middle-class young women could now 'attend a large school where girls are specially trained ... and made capable of becoming clerks, cashiers and ticket-sellers at railway stations ... printing, hairdressing and possibly watch-making'.

That salvation lay in handicrafts, as opposed to the 'evils' of machinery, as preached by Mr William Morris and his Pre-Raphaelite Brotherhood, was not an opinion shared by the writer in *The Englishwoman's Domestic Journal*. 'Perhaps the best thing that has happened to the poor needlewoman (*when we hear of sixteen hours stitching for fourpence*, we may well despair) is the introduction of the sewing machine; employers give 12s. a week for the management of each machine. We have no doubt that ... the sewing machines will ultimately multiply a hundredfold the employment and the wages of all connected with them.'

Vol. XIII.—No. 630.]     JANUARY 23, 1892.     [Price One Penny.

## PINCUSHIONS.

Perhaps there are few articles that lend themselves to such infinite variety as pin-cushions; and yet though they are always with us in vast numbers, they change their fashions almost as quickly as our hats do. That so useful an article should change as to shape and colouring partly arises from their making being an easy and a pleasant employ-ment both for old and young, and partly from the cushion getting dirty and being thrown away, and having to be replaced, and the restless spirit of the time forbidding any renewal of any shape already well known.

About the square and solid bedroom cushion, whose foundation is of coloured batiste, and washable cover of Irish crochet or fine lace, we have not much to say; the change that such a cushion needs is easily given by the variety of the ribbon bows that ornament it, or by the introduction of folds and puffings of pale blue, yellow, or pink Liberty silks amongst the frills of lace or crochet edgings. It is with the ornamental drawing-room pincushions that the greatest taste is required and the newest shapes introduced.

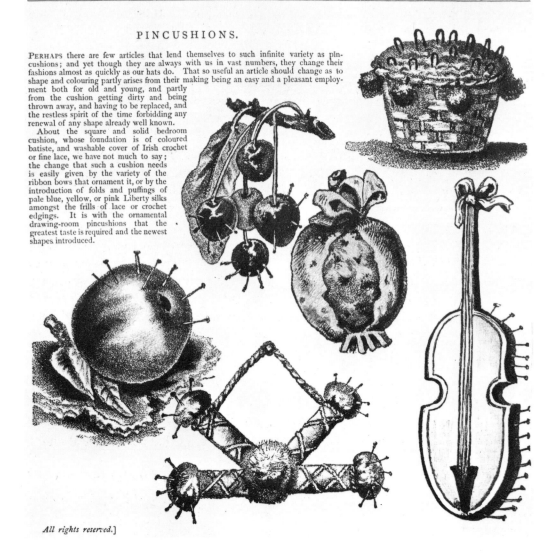

72

Prophesies that 'women will arise from their long sleep of idleness and work out for themselves an independent and honourable position' were a recurring theme of this and other contemporary women's magazines.

'Is it reasonable to expect one branch of the family, merely on account of sex, to be forever giving way, giving up and sitting still, when the others, possessed of no greater faculties, are encouraged to enter the arena, gather strength, renown, money . . .

'. . . at a given period the boys, who until that hour have not evinced the slightest superiority, are removed and enter upon a course of study. The girls . . . remain in the lowlands of elementaries for three or four years more . . . after which they are advanced in the prettiness of "accomplishments"—with the results that thousands upon thousands of women in England . . . are the most pitiable of all created beings.'

Women, the writer urged 'should associate . . . but . . . it is not meant that womanhood should so far forget the characteristic of her sex, *modesty. It is not intended that she should convene public meetings and outrage decency by platform harrangues on the Rights of Women.'*

So what were women, particularly 'the crabbed old maids attached to families as hangers-on, a trouble to brothers, wives, and a torment to young members', to do? The bugle-call dwindles to a penny-whistle squeak with suggestions that they 'could attend lectures given in London and Brighton by the Ladies Association for the Diffusion of Sanitary Knowledge'.

Fiction, as always, interpreted the social scene. Dickens, Thackeray, Mrs Gaskell, George Elliot, the Bröntes and the women's magazines' authors reflected a narrowness, snobbishness, cruelty and vindictiveness of a degree now unthinkable. What modern girl would marry an unwanted suitor for fear that 'his desire for jealous revenge would expose her to the scorn of the world as a girl who had suffered rejected love'? And who today would feel 'scorn' rather than sympathy for such a girl? Other Victorian phenomena such as the ability to faint, blush, or burst into tears occur throughout their women's magazine fiction. A father's snobbery bedevils the heroine of Jane Austen's *Persuasion* and a similar theme predominates in the story 'Love and Hate' in the *Englishwoman's Domestic Magazine*, 1858, in which a typical Victorian father is depicted in full spate, complete with 'Pshaws' and curses.

' "Good heavens, a peasant's son aspire to my daughter's hand! . . . Pshaw! This is folly! If Frances dares to disobey me, on her head be the punishment, and my curse!"

"Silence, Henry! What? Curse your own child?"

"Yes, a thousand times, if she dares to set my commandment at defiance and wed this plebian scamp! Pshaw! Sooner than she should marry that man I would rather see Frances in her grave!" '

Rivalling this and other periodicals in the affections of their readership, was *The Lady*, brought out by Thomas Gibson Bowles (M.P. for King's Lynn 1899–1906), and still going strong. It began as a women's newspaper, its first edition, 19 February 1885 carrying a front page crammed with small ads including those

offering: 'An infallible remedy for colds, stiff necks, sore throats, neuralgia, nerves, rough skin, endorsed by authors, authoresses, actors, actresses, judges, barristers, lawyers, M.P.s, singers, Beauties of the Season, weary hostesses, lecturers, clergymen, travellers by rail, travellers by sea, and those resident in hot climates.' The miracle panacea was named Eucalyptera, and cost 2s. 9d. a bottle.

*The Lady* aimed 'to present information without dullness, and entertainment without vulgarity. . . . It will be written in the English tongue . . . the subjects . . . will be treated from an English point of view.' Among the information it imparted was: 'Mr Parnell will shortly lead to the altar a young American lady. . . . The bride elect is said to be very wealthy.' Instead he created the scandal of the day by falling in love with the already married Kitty O'Shea. It was also noted that Mr Mark Twain 'intends visiting England in May' and that 'Mr Whistler [in the course of a lecture] shifts and shuffles and speaks with a pronounced American accent'. (26 Feb. 1885.)

Fashion dictated: 'For country wear the tailor-made dress is invaluable. The lady of the house may appear in it at the breakfast table . . . to call on poor pensioners, give orders in shops, or for a country stroll, or shooting party . . . to visit stable or kennel. For London wear on damp days it is also appropriate. For boating, coaching or travelling it has no equal.'

A snide wedding report related: 'The Duchess is magnificently tall, quite a head and shoulder above her husband, but he seemed . . . happy as he led her down the aisle. The Duchess is reputed to be very wealthy.'

Other observations included: 'The umbrella should not be regarded as a protection against the weather. It cannot be carried at a size sufficient for this purpose. An umbrella will protect the velvet or satin trimmings or feathers of a bonnet, but nothing more . . . the handle is more important than any other consideration.'

It was also reassuring to know that: 'The Duke of Wellington hunted regularly when he was in Spain; and our soldiers and sailors play cricket whether they are forging their way northwards through the foes and icebergs . . . or fighting our battles under a vertical sun.'

As usual, the small ads provide an insight into everyday life.

'Young lady wants cheap, handsome, healthy bullfinch or robin. Must be tame and come to hand.'

'Mrs Abbott has a lovely Indian tablecloth for sale, brought lately from Delhi.'

And one which might have been captioned 'when the singing had to stop' . . . 'Lady will exchange good music for baby's clothes.'

Deafness was 'cured' by Sims Patent Botanical Distillation complete with 'testimonial from Royalty'. And the 'Vowel Washing Machine' could be tried 'for a month . . . free of expense . . . Every housekeeper or housewife will see that a few simple directions . . . are attended by her servants.' 'Venetian liquid enamel powder' ensured that 'ladies using this preparation need not submit to the expensive process known as enamelling'.

# CHAPTER SIX

# *Needles and Pins*

MARY WOLLSTONECROFT, deploring the futile pursuits of the women of her class and generation in 1792, might have wept, could she have foreseen those of their descendants eighty-nine years later in 1871.

In an age rife with poverty, disease and social injustice, readers of *The Young Englishwoman* were enjoined to devote their energies to creating a plethora of useless objects. Watch-pockets shaped like beetles. Ornamental album covers. Embroidered eye-glass cases. Braided dinner napkins. Embroidered handkerchief boxes. Candlestick ornaments. Crocheted doormats. Ornamental flowerpot covers. Crocheted garters. Embroidered medallions for cigars. Netting and embroidered borders for over-shoes. Ornamental washstand covers. To name but a few.

Pride of place in the forty-eight new women's periodicals published between 1880 and 1900 went to the pin-cushion, an object apparently in fact, fiction and drama indispensable to eloping daughters and/or truant wives. To what else could they have secured those 'forgive me and forget me' notes? 'New models' appeared regularly.

'They have run through several seasons in varying forms. The roses follow the fashion of last year. . . . Just lately . . . I saw pin-cushions made from knitting! . . . People are beginning to put small velvet cushions into napkin rings, thus turning them into fashionable pin-cushions!'

What they did with all those pins, remains a mystery. Were they perhaps, the staple diet of the 'little dressmakers' (living inevitably 'round the corner') who, with mouthfuls between clenched teeth crawled around Madame's voluminous hem-lines?

As always, recently passé fashions were the butt of a younger generation. 'We cannot refrain from laughter at the picture of our mothers and grandmothers with crop heads, and waists to their armpits . . . the portrait painters must have been caricaturists, wilfully exaggerating the hideous costumes to show us what freaks fashion is capable of.'

The fashionable crinoline meanwhile, with its propensity to shoot up when a girl sat down proved a gift to contemporary cartoonists like Phil May, of *Punch* fame.

Battles between 'bonnets and chignons' and 'Catogen versus the American coiffure' aroused a partisanship equalled only by those of rival political factions. 'The coterie against the chignon is very large, but the present voluminous style of coiffure is also supported by a numerous powerful party.' 'At the Court Ball at

Brussels . . . war was waged between the Catogen style of hairdressing, and the so-called American Coiffure, viz. brushed up to the top of the head, and piled in curls . . . leaving the fringe in front.' (*The Lady*, 1885.)

'Impropriety of dressing' was sharply censured. 'For the daily walk, black costumes will be appropriate, but a little caution must be used . . . for to show through the fabric, even the whitest necks and arms, is not ladylike. *Shall every passer-by, every idler, admire or laugh at the necks and arms of young Englishwomen? I do not think anything more is required to point out the impropriety of such dressing.*' Other instructions required that: 'Young girls . . . to be presented at a Court Levée must wear white; white tarletan, white crape, white net skirts worn over silk, satin or moiré petticoats. Nothing is so pretty for young girls as rich white glace silk trains and petticoats, and tulle. . . . The tulle petticoats are made . . . very bouffante, with plaited flounce or puffings at the bottom . . . and bows at the front . . . the train being kept to one side by bunches of ribbons and white flowers. Everyone must of course wear plumes and lappets in the hair.'

Some items conjure less enchanting visions: 'Recorded deaths in this week's cholera epidemic were 1,127.' (*The Queen*, 1861.) 'I should feel obliged if you would give me information as to how fleas can be kept from a sickbed.' (*The Queen*, 26 June 1869.)

Cleanliness, as John Wesley (1703–1791) had preached, was next to godliness, yet a bath, like marriage, was not 'to be undertaken lightly'. 'The most fitting time to take a bath is when the body is gently excited by exercise, then the bath does not give a headache. Before breakfast is a good time . . . but most people prefer the afternoon. The bath should be entered about two and a half hours after a lightish meal, at which a fair quantity of liquid with a small amount of stimulant has been taken, and after a short, brisk walk, sufficient to induce a slight perspiration.'

Cheap liquor made 'stimulants' a national problem. The drunken swell was a stock music-hall character. Among the 'lower orders' drink accounted for more despair than it was designed to relieve. For the lower middle, and middle classes striving to maintain a precarious foot on the social or employment ladder, a lapse could prove disastrous. Efforts to combat alcoholism induced thousands to 'sign the pledge' and flock to the ranks of the Salvation Army founded by General Booth in Whitechapel in 1865.

*The Family Friend* (October 1878, price 1d.) campaigned: 'Use all your influence to close those curses of our land, the drinking saloons . . . urge your sons and daughters never to taste the intoxicating cup. Never let your son accuse, 'Mother, it was at your table I learned the drink that has been my ruin.'' '

Somewhat unusually for a women's magazine, *Hand and Hearth* (1876) covered a murder trial; that of the mysterious death of a Mr Bravo in 1876 which became a *cause celèbre*. Mrs Bravo's alleged use of the arsenical compound from soaked fly-papers for cosmetic purposes, and Mr Bravo's equally common Victorian addiction to laudanum left the verdict of murder or suicide unresolved.

Charles Bravo had been young, athletic. Commented *Hand and Hearth* — 'Today

everyone is athletic. If he cannot bicycle, he can cricket, run or wrestle, row or throw. Ladies swim and ladies row, but ladies very wisely keep clear of the cricket field.'

Even cricket was not always 'cricket'. 'There is no reason' comments the editor, 'why a young man, directly he belongs to a village cricket club should begin to talk slang, wear his hat on one side, go to the public house, smoke a dirty pipe, make his mother weep . . . and his sister blush . . . and show in other ways that he is becoming more of an animal than a man.'

Across the Channel they were more preoccupied with the Franco-Prussian War and with hunger. A report from *The Young Englishwoman*'s correspondent, 'sent by balloon post' tells us: 'So difficult . . . is it to get meat that cooks of good families . . . have to stand with hundreds of other persons for hours, and take their turn for admission into the shop. In some instances the women begin to congregate around the butchers' shops at night, remaining until they are open. . . . No one is allowed to buy more than 100 grammes.'—all a great trial, especially when, as *The Young Englishwoman*'s fashion writer complained: 'Every day should produce some striking novelty, some elegant design . . . but because of the disturbances the modes are by no means as varied this season.'

Some styles met with censure: 'Princess Louise . . . wore a black tulle dress trimmed with folds of green tulle at the bodice. I notice that she, as well as the Duchess of Edinburgh wear their ball dress bodices cut off the shoulders . . . but I am glad to say this ugly fashion is peculiar to them.'

Dress which made life easier for women seems always to have met with suspicion. 'Short dresses, or "costumes" . . . when they first made their appearance were ignored by the British matron, who looked upon the wearers with the superiority of concious virtue . . . and continued to gather her own dress in great bunches under each arm. If her husband was with her . . . his boots were dragged in a muddy train . . . and his anger kindled by the times his wife's dress was trodden upon. The short dress has long been worn in France and America, but here it was called "fast", and a woman who wore one suspected of being no better than she ought to be.'

There was also 'bad news for English ladies from abroad. Continental salons and ballrooms are being closed against them. English ladies dress so shabbily that they spoil the room.'

Other reasons brought ex-patriots home. 'Many people, owing to . . . the earthquake in Nice, have left the Continent. However . . . it is an ill wind that blows nobody any good . . . in the case of Lady Randolf Churchill's mother, Mrs Jerome. Reported to have suffered from paralysis for some years, she had become entirely bedridden, till terrified by the shock of the earthquake, she sprang from bed . . . since when she has recovered the use of her limbs.'

Holidays, abroad or at home, were strictly for the wealthy. The Bank Holiday Act (1871) gave ordinary people the chance of a day out on Hampstead Heath, or later to Epping Forest, presented to the nation by Queen Victoria in 1882. And parks, that happiest of Victorian inventions, known as 'the poor man's drawing room', became part of the urban scene. As *The Queen* records during the 1880s: 'It is understood that her Majesty will, early in the present season, pay a visit to the East End of London for the purpose of seeing Victoria Park, the park of the people.'

'While strolling through the park one day . . .' the ordinary girl might well have had a livelier time than her upper-class sister at a grand garden party, as a reply in the Answers to Correspondents column in *The Queen* admits: 'Marjorie: There is no help for it; even at grand garden parties, men have been absent. They do not appear to care for women's society unless the bait of an heiress is dangled. We cannot help it, but only wish it were otherwise.'

Dinner party, 1890.

Some men had less choice. ' A singular statement' . . . made at a meeting of Bromley Kent Board of Guardians, 1881, records: 'It has been customary for the Board to allow ladies to attend the Workhouse to read to the inmates. . . . On one occasion a lady brought three others with her, one of whom carried a cat on her shoulders, and the quartet sang hymns to the elderly men when the latter were impatiently expecting their dinner. . . . Another lady visited the lying-in ward, and in stentorian tones told the mothers of the newly-born babies, that they were doomed.'

Whether she referred to the mothers or their babies, or both, is uncertain. The infant mortality rate prompted the question in *The Ladies Domestic Magazine* (1880) 'Have we ever asked ourselves how it happens that one out of every five children born in London is carried to an early grave?'

'Until a few years ago', it continues, 'London was the only capital in the Christian world without a hospital for sick children. Between five and six years ago, a few benevolent individuals exerted themselves to found a hospital for children only. . . . A house was taken in Great Ormond Street, Queen Square, that had once been a Nobleman's mansion. Nothing could be better calculated for this purpose . . .'

Beyond the capital, conditions remained unchanged: 'If anyone wants to know what poverty means, she should go among the shirtmakers in slack times. The women are round the warehouse door before it opens, on a cold winter's morning in Milcaster. One morning there were twenty-three of us. . . . The forewoman looked ready to cry. 'I have only three bundles to give out', she said. 'Twenty went away . . . not knowing where their next meal was coming from. Even in good times', the narrator relates, 'she got no more than 4d. a dozen for making complete shirts, from six in the morning till ten at night.' (*Young Englishwoman*, 1869.)

No evidence exists that readers of *The Ladies Magazine* wished to know about poverty in Milcaster on a cold winter's morning, or any other time. More exciting events were afoot, such as '. . . the Parisian society wedding on which £20,000 was said to have been spent on festivals alone. Presents were displayed . . . representing more than two million pounds worth of precious stones. Silver plate worthy of a queen, diamonds enough to exhaust Golconda . . . pearls that would have ruined Cleopatra . . . a Louis XVI parure of sapphire and diamonds valued at £50,000 . . . jewelled combs, diadem, ear-rings, bodice clasps and two bracelets.'

'In glamorous Vienna . . . select balls are at their zenith, and charming belles dames with the light fantastic toe glide along highly polished floor, keeping tune to the bewitching strains of Strauss waltzes.'

And as 'Eyewitness' related in *The Ladies World*, 1887, 'The Duke of Edinburgh's ball was . . . the finest that has ever taken place in Malta. The dance floor . . . was decorated with flags and flowers . . . the harbour was lit with the electric light of all the ships of the fleet.'

Equally important as knowing what went on, where, was knowing who was who. 'Most of us remember the beautiful Constance, Duchess of Westminster, the Duke's first wife. She succeeded to the high position of leader of Society, held in the early days of Queen Victoria, by her mother, the Duchess of Sunderland. She was widely mourned and regarded as irreplaceable.'

But not, it seems, by the Duke. Referring to Constance's successor as 'the subject of this article' the writer concedes: 'She provides Grosvenor House, Eaton Hall and Cliveden with a chatelaine . . . equipped for her great position. It must be mentioned', she adds, 'that her brother, the present Lord Chesham, had married the Duke's daughter, Beatrice. Her sisters are the Countess of Leicester and Lady Lyttleton.'

Not everyone could be a wealthy Parisian bride, or a duchess. Keeping up with the Joneses often meant 'deprivation'. 'It is notorious that women of the middle class, to meet the demands of finery . . . have voluntarily relinquished the comfort of an additional servant, and descended to servile drudgery.'

Acquiring or exchanging 'finery' or necessities was increasingly met by the use of the For Sale and Exchange columns of *The Queen*.

Five minutes with this therapeutic hairbrush was guaranteed to cure headaches, while little more was apparently needed to halt baldness itself . . . 'Fraudulent imitations' were pronounced 'utterly worthless'.

'Antimacassar : I have a handsome antimacassar, worked in double-Berlin wool, I want in exchange a bogwood necklace with Irish diamonds, or a pair of Searles ear-tops.'

'I wish for a sandlewood fan, also Bohemian garnet ornaments, also opal, garnet, turquoise "regard" rings.'

There was no predicting what those lady-like Victorian girls might keep, if not up their sleeves, then within their muffs:

'I have a six-barrelled revolver, pocket-pistol for sale, very small and beautifully finished.'

'Brace of pistols required.'

And was it some earlier, reformed Annie Oakley who announced: 'I have a first-rate double-barrelled gun by Greener, muzzle load, worth £10. To be exchanged for a sewing machine.'

Desperation seems to cry aloud from the words: 'I still have my large, rich plum cake covered with ornamental icing, weighing 14 lbs. What will anyone offer me for it? I have also jet ornaments, bloodstone brooches, long ostrich feathers, gilt hair ornaments, pencil cases, writing boxes, and six yards of tatting edges.'

Ambiguity creeps in with unconscious humour:

'I have a seagull's hat, very pretty bird in front.'

'I have a very handsome gentleman's Indian gold ring worth £5.'

'I have a curious Cross made by a Russian prisoner with a plaster face, hare skin, recently dressed.'

'I have a squirrel skin, whole body, head and tail, mounted to trim hat.'

More practical types wanted to exchange 'a fine copy in oils of Mrs Siddons for a turning lathe'; 'a handsome gold bracelet, a diamond and emerald ring . . . for a good lawn mower.'

Those wishing to employ, rather than 'relinquish the comforts of' servants, were advised that:

'Characters of servants must be honest, sober, clean, industrious, neat, tidy, regular, systematic. . . . If a cook, ask particulars of soups, roasting and boiling, pastry, care and economy. If a nurse, look for a quiet temperament, kindness, watching care and experience. If a lady's maid, clever at hairdressing and dressmaking, discreet and quiet.

'The lady's maid has also to take up her mistress's early morning tea, keep her underclothes in order, air and place it ready in the morning, see that . . . changes of dress are laid out . . . before her mistress requires them. She must dress and undress her, brush and dress her hair, shop for her, nurse her when she is ill. Be quick and correct in the art of cutting out and making dresses, plain sewing, and keeping her acquaintance with different styles up to date.

'We may remark that those households are best conducted where the mistress never converses with her servants . . . but to give an order, ask a question, say good morning or good evening to her maids.'

The *Ladies Treasury*, first published in 1870, outlined a more spartan regime for the mistress of the house.

'A good mistress will rise at seven oclock. . . . She will ring for her kettle or tea-urn. . . . Breakfast over, the mistress brushes her husband's and sons' hats. . . . She then goes downstairs and orders dinner. She then goes upstairs and assists in making the beds. The washing should be "put out" when one servant alone is kept. Otherwise the damping, folding and ironing is done by the mistress, and the hard labour by the maid. *But no lady should attempt to have the whole of the washing done at home.* . . . We may mention that it is always desirable that a lady's hands should look white and nice.'

No such mundane problems preoccupied readers of *The Queen*.

'Will an income of £800 a year admit of our keeping five servants . . . and having a

An illustration typifying the male chauvinist attitude met by Victorian women seeking outlets outside the home confines.

brougham during the Season? Family consists of self, husband and three children under six years of age.'

'Time off' and 'followers' for servants was a recurring, vexed question. 'My servants', wrote 'Celia', 'three in number, demand a weekly half-holiday . . . and visits from their young men. Do you think I should agree to this?' Emphatically she is told: 'On no account must Celia agree to the unreasonable exactions of her servants. I allow each of mine to attend Church once on Sundays. I strictly forbid friends and followers. I allow a day out once in six or eight weeks, as may be convenient. *It is a bad thing to give servants too much liberty. They are seldom grateful.*'

Debarred from any social life, the girls 'downstairs' could solace themselves with *Home Notes* (1870), the *Girl's Own Paper* (1880) and *Home Chat* (1895). The tone used towards this penny-a-week readership proved in striking contrast to that of earlier magazines. So far from grovelling to 'delight and please the Fair', editorial dictates resembled those of the grimmer species of headmistress, or custodians of Homes for Recalcitrant Females. Inevitably romantic queries predominated: 'It is unseemly and vulgar . . . to send Valentines to young men. We can only wonder . . . that so many mothers have neglected to teach their daughters to be modest and retiring.'

Contrary to popular legend, it seems it was Mama, rather than Papa, to whom trembling suitors applied.

'Your would-be intended did wrong in not asking permission to pay his addresses

84

to you. You should have said "Ask my mother's permission before I can consider your suit." '

'Did you actually receive a proposal . . . without your mother's consent? You should have declined with indignation without her prior permission.'

Teenage romance gained scant approval. 'At eighteen you are far too young to receive the addresses of any man. You have duties to your mother to fulfil at home for years yet, before the idea of marrying should enter your head.'

Not that Mama's judgment was always beyond reproach. 'It would be foolish . . . even to consider this man's proposal. . . . He probably belongs to the lower class of Socialist sceptics. I am astonished that your Mama should have bestowed her approval on this undesirable suitor!'

How girls ever became engaged or married, remains a mystery. 'It is utterly unseemly, and as much as your reputation is worth, to walk at night with any man, but your father or brother. You must always be accompanied by a friend, if walking, even in daylight, with a man to whom you are not engaged. Never walk alone with strange men, even if properly introduced. Always have a female friend with you.'

Men, especially strange men, were an alarming species, best avoided. Yet satire, to be effective, must emphasise a truth. Other than in the inflamed imaginations of old maids of both sexes, ham dramatists and hack writers, did these moustache-twirling, mercenary, seduce-at-the-drop-of-a-top-hat villains ever exist? Current literature and every women's magazine's correspondence column suggest they did. The Victorian girl, kept in darkest ignorance about sex, nurtured on impossible ideals, romantic slush, was easy prey for the unscrupulous, scheming, or merely vain male predator. In such circumstances 'the preservation of personal beauty' recommended in *The Toilet* of 1843, could prove more of a liability than an asset to the girl in the basement in 1892. Her attempts to improve her looks met with scant approval from the editor of *The Girl's Own Annual*.

'Elsie, a housemaid, writes that she is afflicted with a nose which is short, thick and flat. She submits to our judgment whether it would render this feature more shapely were she to wear a pair of glove-stretchers at night so that it might not stand in her way when trying to get a situation as a housemaid. Great plainness might stand in her way as a parlour-maid, lady's maid or nurse, but as a cook or housemaid would not signify. Leave your nose alone', she is told, 'and be thankful that you have one!'

'It is both unbecoming and injurious to dye the hair, and hideous for a young girl to wear a wig. Wear instead a frank smile.'

Attempts to step out of social line met with withering discouragement.

'Abandon the notion of becoming a governess. You might offer yourself as a mother's help, or do domestic work.'

'We scarcely think your parents would oppose your marrying a respectable young man. But if the man is a *gentleman* your parents show wisdom in regarding an unequal match with apprehension.'

Such strictures were for 'below stairs'. The rise in population following the Industrial Revolution created a newly-rich lower-middle-class society for whom

A new career
for the
Victorian girl.

fear of committing a social solecism was an ever-present nightmare. For the wives and daughters of newly established tradesmen and manufacturers, the *Girl's Own Paper* was at hand with a guide through the complicated cat's-cradle of Victorian etiquette.

'Stand until the lady of the house on whom you are calling, comes in. When asked your name, say Mrs or Miss, as the case may be.'

'As a rule, bow only; but were the stranger a relation or old friend of the family, it would be more gracious to offer your hand.'

'When shown into a private reception room, and the lady of the house is not there, but a stranger, make a slight bow, but take no further notice.'

'If you take muffins with afternoon tea, you had better take your gloves off, unless you particularly want to spoil them!'

Never for an instant was the editorial oracle at a loss. She knew 'how to play a zither', could instruct on 'how to knit stockings for deep-sea fishermen' or on 'the pretty art of skeletonising leaves', 'painting on chamois leather', or correct pronunciation—'An harmonium, is the way it should be referred to'. Readers were told, 'You must clean your cockatoo by rubbing him with a little flour'; 'At fourteen your dress should come to the top of your boots'; 'You should take a feather boa if you expect to be out after sunset'; 'the best dress for a walking tour is serge'; 'a

Jackdaw is not a vegetable'; 'a child of twelve has no right to read novels'; 'the exclamation "O Lor!" is both profane and vulgar.'

A mother of a forward child is 'reassured': 'Because your child gives evidence of precocious ability you should . . . endeavour to keep him back. A child's brain is quite soft until the age of seven. Among the Ancients we find precocity almost invariably followed by early death. From our own personal observation we know a boy and girl who both died at seven years old.'

Her disapproval was monumental and all-embracing.

'We hold the intensive realism in the modern theatre is utterly subversive to the principles of Art.'

'We have no hesitation in saying that the literature of the age is thoroughly degraded.'

'Modern society is vulgarised. The retired shopkeeper who can drop his thousands as easily as his aitches, lords it over the blue blood of the Plantagenets'— which, since the Plantagenets died out around 1499, was no light feat.

But if personal beauty in the basement 'didn't signify', it was all-important in the drawing room. Consulting *The Queen* (1861), the reader could discover that:

'Avicomis fluid has the astonishing power of imparting a rich golden shade to hair of any colour.'

'Kleo's Bloom of Lilies imparts a beautiful permanent whiteness to the complexion.'

She could . . . 'send for the eye-brightener as used by the Empress of Morocco, the Queen of Fiji and a dozen other Potentates.' And assisting nature was no longer 'degraded'. As a small ad testified, 'Bloomine lends an innocent rose colour to the cheeks.'

Not surprisingly in an age when cholera, typhoid, typhus, consumption and a dozen other now curable diseases made death, not so much 'a welcome guest' as an entrenched, uninvited resident, women's magazine fiction was steeped in funereal gloom. Even the heroine's happiest moments were descanted by dire forebodings.

'Esther!' He snatched her to his heart, his lips pressed hers. 'Speak!' he urged. 'Do you love me?' 'Yes', she answered. 'But something tells me it is a love which will bring nothing but sorrow and death. Do I go to happiness or sorrow?' (*Ladies Treasury*, 1887.)

In the 'subversive' theatre of the day, Ibsen, Oscar Wilde's and Bernard Shaw's New Women knew exactly where they were going. One had even penetrated *The Englishwoman's Magazine*. Chapter VIII of 'An Old fashioned Girl' 1871 opens:

' "What do you think Polly is going to do this winter?" asked Fanny.

"Going to lecture on Women's Rights?" exclaimed the young gentleman.'

Girls, it seemed, were 'getting above themselves'. Complained a letter in an issue of *The Queen*, that year: 'There is no end to the . . . ingenuity with which women seek for new employment. Hundreds of women emigrate because they can get no work. Scores . . . think it excuse enough for sinking into degradation for want of food. Girls whose parents were content to keep a little shop, are now educated to read

French, and strum Schumann, with minds too lofty for healthy, wholesome housework.' It was signed, Viscountess Strangford.

Deplorable though it appeared to the Viscountess that women emigrated or fell 'into degradation' over trifles like unemployment and starvation, it had occurred to others that there might be alternatives to 'servile drudgery' (as applied to the middle-class woman) and/or 'wholesome healthy housework' (as re-defined for working-class girls). *Our Own Gazette* of April 1884 records: 'Telephone offices have opened a . . . congenial and profitable sphere to ladies, not only as a means of obtaining . . . remuneration, but also for developing business habits and ideas which are of no small value to women.'

The new instrument received a mixed reception: 'There are stories of invalid ladies who . . . telephone their doctors at night. We have heard of doctors who positively refuse . . . a telephone being put in their house, as the consequences might be serious.'

The Victorian home was described by Bernard Shaw as 'the woman's workhouse and the girl's prison'. By hook or by crook they were determined to break free.

'The question of employing women as commercial travellers is exercising the minds of warehousemen. In the City warehouses, women already hold responsible positions as buyers, as well as saleswomen and have proved themselves excellent 'men of business'. (*The Lady*, 1885.)

'No less a person than Her Gracious Majesty has become Patroness of a Society designed to assist girls to trades . . . glass-engraving, ivory carving, ladies cutters, and hairdressing. The work is valuable, inasmuch as girls and women are capable of undertaking occupations other than housework, needlework and governessing.' (*The Lady*, 1885.)

It was a step forward in terms of equal opportunity—but not of equality of reward: 'The great pressure of candidates . . . makes women ready to accept lower terms than men. This is shown . . . where women compete on equal terms with men. Yet female authors, artists, singers are paid as well as male persons . . .'

Thanks to Florence Nightingale, nursing was now a respectable profession. As *The Girl's Own Paper* announced: 'At the London Hospital, both Ladies and women of the lower classes may be received without payment, and will be paid £12 the first year and £20 the second. Candidates are required to be between twenty-five and forty years.'

But a *lady doctor*? 'Great heavens, can you imagine any modest woman advertising herself as a *medical practitioner*? A woman who enters upon the study of medicine must inevitably lose all the charms and refined sentiments which so gracefully adorn her sex. *She must renounce all claims to the name of woman.*' (*The Lady*, 1885.)

As far back as 1869 *The Young Englishwoman* indicated the animosity encountered by would-be women doctors, not only from their own sex, but from the allegedly 'fair-minded' male. 'Miss J. Blake and four other ladies . . . at Edinburgh University . . . commenced the study of medicine. For one session things went smoothly, then the professors refused to teach the women. The male students mobbed them. The authorities said . . . they could no longer permit their presence in the university. . . . Three of the most eminent physicians in London have resigned . . . rather than examine women in obstetrics.'

More liberal counsels prevailed in Ireland where—'on the 10th of last month they passed a resolution opening their examinations to women.' (*The Queen*.) In England, 'after appeals in Parliament, the Royal Free Hospital (London) admitted women. It is the only place in England where women can graduate in medicine.' (*The Lady*.)

'For a woman whose sole ambition is to obtain a husband, no career is possible . . . she must become the slave which men for generations have selfishly endeavoured to make her. But there are women with a loftier ideal, who desire to do good in the world; for such, I think, medicine is a profitable study.' (*The Lady*, 1871.) That any more 'lofty ideal' existed than ministering to the comforts of a husband, was a near blasphemous statement to most males. But male apoplexy surely reached its apotheosis in the pronouncement of a Victorian father who declared: '*I would rather see a daughter of mine in her coffin than in the dissecting room!*' Nor could male chauvinism have been more succinctly expressed than in the 'final word' of the editor of *The Lady*: 'Loving, or being made love to, is the English girl's destiny. Like the sensible girl she is, she submits to it with surprisingly good grace.'

Other editorial chairs were impressively occupied. Oscar Wilde edited *Woman's World* (no connection with a recently published magazine of that name), Arnold Bennett edited *Woman* (again no connection with today's periodical), Frank Harris presided over *Hearth and Home*.

*The Young Englishwoman* proclaimed: 'A new era has arrived . . . to make women free and independent . . . to teach them to do and dare in the battle of life.'

Doing and daring needed courage. 'Everybody at home thought I had lost my head when I began to talk of going to college', wrote a reader to *The Lady* in 1871. The college was Newnham, Cambridge, founded that year. Oxford followed suit seven years later with Lady Margaret Hall, Somerville and St Anne's (1879), St Hugh's 1886 and St Hilda's (1895). A St Hugh's student records in *Woman's World*, 1887: 'There is a . . . notion that there must be something queer about a college for women, and the women who go there; or that none go, save such as are lacking in morals, or that a desire for eccentricity alone leads women to desert the beaten track of domestic life. We cannot anticipate that women's colleges will cease to be mysterious to the outside world until it is generally recognised that it is desirable that women's lives should cease to stagnate in the round of personal loves.'

Old conditioning, nevertheless, died hard. 'I found newcomers like myself entertained by Miss —— who did the honours while knitting rapidly. . . . Miss —— makes all the socks for her family of eight brothers, knitting in term-time a pair a fortnight.'

A former student writing to *The Lady* in 1871 recalls, 'I looked mechanically for the bell, thinking I should like a servant to help me unpack. I discovered later that only the mistress and resident lecturers have a bell in their rooms. *Finding that I was*

EVERY ARTICLE MARKED IN PLAIN FIGURES. & NO ABATEMENT MADE OR DISCOUNT ALLOWED.

ALL GOODS TO BE PAID FOR WHEN PURCHASED OR UPON DELIVERY.

The electro-plating department of Benetfink and Fox, 1800s.

*completely thrown on my own resources, I knelt down by one of my trunks . . . and dropped a few tears.'*

'Unable to face a dining-hall full of girls, I turned and rushed back to my room and burst into tears. I found afterwards that Freshmen often get very little to eat for days, so difficult is it for them to look after themselves. With girls who have seen nothing of the world, this timidity lasts for some time, and they are really half-starved at first.' Scarcely a picture of the hatchet-faced 'blue-stockings' men so enjoyed denigrating.

'Working the female brain' it seems, was not without hazards. Declared the *Girl's Own Annual* in 1892: 'Women students have generally extreme sensibility of nerves . . . irritability of temper. They are more liable to attacks of disease. Over-study causes a kind of dullness of the brain.' While a reader who complained of 'a red hot face' was told—'it is probably attributable to working the brain too soon after meals.'

*The Young Englishwoman* daringly urged its readers to submit to these risky proceedings. In an article entitled 'How Men can Stimulate the Intellectual Life of

Women' it conceded: 'Mental culture should not, and does not as a rule, rob women of her womanliness, nor render her less lovable. A husband might encourage his wife in a suitable choice of reading matter. He could read the paper aloud to her while she darns his socks.'

That, the sock-darning excluded, the process might be reversed, occurred to at least one reader: 'If working women realised how closely the welfare of the working classes is interwoven in current political questions, they would take more interest in politics. Although possessing no direct power ... they can exercise an immense influence over their husbands and sons.'

Women were also struggling free from their whalebone stays, their dragging skirts. 'All that is required is a little courage' *Woman's World* campaigned. And moral courage, whether in the form of cycling in the new Mrs Bloomer style breeches, or supporting the Rational Dress Movement, was not lacking.

The objects of the Rational Dress Movement, as reported by *Woman's World*, were: 'To protest against any fashion ... which deforms the figure, impedes movement of the body, or injures health. To protest against corsets, tight-fitting bodices, high and narrow-heeled boots or shoes; against heavily weighted skirts that strain the dorsal regions; tie-down cloaks, crinolettes and crinolines of any shape as deforming, indecent and vulgar. ... To recommend ... the maximum weight of underclothing should not exceed 7 lbs; that it should consist of two garments only, one, woollen combinations, and the celebrated divided skirt.'

Fashion writers in this magazine continued with pronouncements such as 'Brocatelle has come to the fore. Matelesse is the fabric of the year. Boas are expected to continue in favour. ...'

Etiquette—the depths of one's decollete in relation to the number of one's servants, what it was 'proper' to eat with, or put on the chiffonier—was as rigidly observed as ever. The *Young Englishwoman* recorded in 1871:

'No lady with a modest menage of only two servants, should be décolleté at dinner.

'At dinner parties at home, the hostess should not wear a low dress; the same style of dress is suitable for quiet dinners abroad, but for three weeks' invitations, she must be décolleté.'

'Aimee presents her compliments and would feel obliged if she could be informed if it is considered vulgar to eat shrimps with the fingers?'

'Bertha writes: Will you kindly let me know if it is proper to put glass and decanters and tea and coffee services on a chiffonier in a drawing-room, when you do not have a dining room?

'Should table-napkins be used at any other meal except dinner? Should carving knife and fork rests be used at supper as well as dinner? I am about to change my position for one a little higher, and should not like to appear ignorant of these little things.'

'Aprons are becoming more and more in favour, but I do not admire little aprons of muslins and ribbons ... they are too soubrette and should be left to housemaids.'

Correct wear for mourning also caused some anxious queries, which *The Young Englishwoman* of 1871 was able to settle with its customary assurance.

Q. Is it proper to wear lace sleeves and collar when in mourning for an aunt or grandmother?

A. No. Muslin or linen alone should be worn. Six months' mourning is required for grandparents.

Q. How long should crape be worn for a parent? I have worn mine for fourteen months.

A. Twelve months is the usual time.

Q. May a crape bonnet or hat be worn for the full period of mourning?

A. Yes, but the whole dress must be in deep mourning to match.

Q. How long should the servants be kept in black when the family will wear it for two years?

A. One year.

Rapidly changing fashions made hanging on to one's clothes pointless. As numerous *Woman's World* small ads testify, long periods of mourning proved not only profitable to dressmakers and milliners, they also provided bargains for less well-to-do readers: 'Mourning. Small lady going into mourning wishes to dispose of scarcely worn dresses, hats, etc.'

Best-selling authors Olive Schreiner and Ouida contributed to *Woman's World*. Posterity has done less than justice to Ouida, whose political insight was shrewd and uncannily prophetic. Of America she predicted: 'Because America has had no war but Civil War, she considers herself safe from any cantagion of battle fever of the massed batallions of Europe. But this security may be a dangerous dream.' Of Africa: 'When a share in the plunder and conquest of Africa is desired, a reason is found for bombardment and blockade.' Of Germany and Russia: 'The brutal despotism of Russia and Germany . . . can bruise and pound . . . cold as stone and dull as lead. Under the excuse of war, the Germans violate every rule of decency, every precept of mercy. The respect for a gallant foe . . . is to them unknown.'

Long before nuclear weapons forced even the most boneheaded of military high-ups to a similar, if reluctant conclusion, she wrote: 'There is no remedy for this disease [war] that can be looked for from any government. The only chance for the disarmament of the world will be the possibility that the game will become so costly that its players will be unable to risk the stakes.'

Ouida died six years before the outbreak of the first world war.

Time and again, *Woman's World*, campaigning for wider opportunities for women, emphasised 'that an honest trade is infinitely more dignified . . . than the genteel poverty which necessitates one long course of cringing to rich relations, and grudging charity.'

Thanks to an American invention, the typewriting machine which, as *The Queen* assured its readers, 'does not overtax the physical or mental abilities of women', marketed by a Mr C. L. Scholes and a Mr Gladden in 1874, an 'honest trade' materialised. It enabled girls not only to break into that erstwhile masculine preserve, the business world, but even, with a measure of hitherto unknown independence, into more august establishments. The *Golden Penny* of 1898 reported that 'In the staid old House of Commons, a very clever lady typewriter has been given a desk, salary and an assistant. When asked by Lord Salisbury to type a letter as she was about to leave, she replied "It was not her place to work overtime for the Premier of England." '

'Sensitive nerves' were still persisting. 'The creaking of boots and shoes, so very disagreeable to sensitive nerves', *Home Notes* advises, 'may be prevented by soaking the bottoms, or having them thoroughly dampened.'

But neither nerves, boots nor spirits were dampened in 1896 at Henley when 'the whole river-reach was frothy with airy frills of transparent muslin and lace. . . .' (From M.A.P.—Mainly About People—16 July 1896, edited by journalist and politician T. P. O'Connor.) A flash of enchantment from the dying century which might have been captured on the 'new hand cameras, price 4s. 6d.' advertised in the same journal.

# CHAPTER SEVEN

## *Progress, Poverty and Pipe-dreams*

THE year 1900 was ushered in optimistically by *The Home Friend*. 'The century just past has a record of progress almost the greatest in the world's history . . . Electricity has become a force never dreamed of . . . look at telephones, telegraphs, wireless telegraphy, railways, steamers, motor cars etc. just beginning . . . the development of civilisation and refinement increase daily.'

In London, the Underground was electrified. The escalator was invented in America. In Germany the first Zeppelin cast its ominous shadow of the shape of things to come. The same year saw the Relief of Mafeking in the wearisome South African war. Queen Victoria died (1901). Edward VII was crowned.

The thirty years following the Compulsory Education Act of 1870 saw the expansion of a new women's magazine market. Their contents were cosy, chatty, and unashamedly escapist. For the 'downstairs' domestic, shop-girl, factory worker, working-class housewife, able to participate vicariously via their pages, in the activites of royalty and the 'gentry' they provided a glamour later supplied by the cinema. Victorian religious class-structured conditioning ensured that the 'lower orders' 'knew their place'; followed with acceptance rather than envy the life of 'their betters'. A lost world of basement kitchens, singing kettles, hissing gas-mantles, rows of bells summoning for duties beyond the green baize door, is recaptured by items in *Home Notes* issues of 1905.

'Queen Amelie, who was born at Twickenham in 1865 . . . has a horror of tight lacing. The first use Her Majesty made of the Rontgen rays was to photograph a lady at Court . . . and thus prove how pernicious the habit is.'

'Just before the Kaiser sets out on a railway journey . . . every stage is minutely examined . . . Signals at night are avoided so as not to disturb the repose of the monarch . . . every conceivable measure is taken to cause the Emperor's journey to pass . . . as easily as possible.'

Entangled royal relationships read like conundrums: 'The son of Princess Letitia, wife of ex-king Amadeus, her uncle, is his mother's first cousin, and is also the grand-nephew to his father. His mother, as the wife of his great uncle, must therefore be his great-aunt, and as Princess Letitia must necessarily be the cousin of her uncle's child, therefore her own son must be second cousin to herself.'

'Prince Oscar of Sweden's consort, who is aunt to the Duchess of Albany, has

now a stronger tie with our own Royal Family. For it was her grandson who recently married Princess Margaret of Connaught. Queen Sophia is also sister to the Grand Duke of Luxenberg, and Prince Nicholas of Nassau. The Queen of the Netherlands is her grand-niece, and among her relatives she reckons the Royal House of Russia.'

Next to being royalty or 'gentry' there was nothing like being very, very, rich. 'Of the many American heiresses who have married European noblemen ... is the young Comtesse de Castellane. She was one of the wealthiest American girls ... when she married the Comte. No sooner had the young Comte married the millions of the Gould family, than ... horses of purest breed were added to his stables, fabulous sums spent on diamonds ... and over the gaming tables. Whole rivers of gold were poured out ... in the way of balloons, submarines, telescopes, newspapers and even circuses.'

Great-grandmothers were as perfect as ever. 'The hurry and scurry of modern life has lowered the old housewifely standard. Imagine the horror of our great-grandmothers, could they see us buying ready-made clothes, prepared foods, etc. The fact remains that no woman today ... can compare with her great grandmother.'

Even when *Home Chat* nose-dived from cloud cuckoo-land it carefully retained its rose-coloured spectacles. Holloway prison is described as 'a charming building,

looking more like a turretted dwelling of Knights and Fair Ladies of the Middle Ages, than a prosaic prison for evil-doers'. In a coy, fashion-reporting style they continue: 'Prison babies wear a uniform dress of black and white check flannel. Lift the hem of the baby garment, and the black arrow of prison is seen stamped on the white flannel petticoats and undergarments.'

Royal babes it seemed, might fare even worse. 'The tiny prince of Piedmont . . . now a year old, is an excellent advertisement for the "hardening process" in which his queen mother believes. He and his sisters begin their day by being taken from their beds and plunged into water which ordinary mortals would find bitterly cold.'

Constantly plugged was the message 'the true woman's horizon is bounded by the four walls of her home, and those four walls shut in or shut out the sun, as he who is her Lord and Master chooses.' And this message was accompanied by ridicule of the New Woman: 'It seems as if the poultry world can boast of suffragettes. A Sussex breeder possesses a hen which . . . last year did not lay but moulted into cock's plumage. *This is an indication of the way the wind is blowing.*' (*Mother and Home*, 1908.)

Letters suggesting that women had invaded all-male smoking carriages had been indignantly refuted by *The Lady* in their issue of 3 May 1894. 'No lady would ever dream of doing such a thing in the presence of the opposite, or even her own sex.'

By 1900 one lady did more than dream of doing it, according to a copy of *The Mascot* (first published 1885). 'The New Woman has got as far as Carlisle. A gentleman recently jumped into a London express at the last moment. He was smoking, and noticing a lady, remarked "I hope you don't object to my smoking?" He says he felt small when she replied, "I don't object to smoking, but I do object to bad cigarettes. Have one of mine." '

Another 'straw in the wind' was the growing popularity of that unladylike pastime—cycling. 'Among the dangers of this sport are cyclist's stare—an expression of nervous anxiety. Cyclist's wrists are caused through gripping the handlebars, cyclist's spine by vibration, and then there is cyclist's eye. However expert a rider may be, he is compelled to keep continual watch. The muscles of the eye become overstrained, *which leads to collapse of the eyeballs* if not attended to.'

Despite repeated insistence that 'a woman's true vocation was to submit to the domination of her husband' doubts were beginning to creep into readers' minds. 'The word obey in the marriage service might have been good enough for our grandmothers . . . but today, love and honour is, to my mind, all that is needed. Obey is a remnant of barbarous days and reminds me of serfdom.' (*The Mascot*, 1903.)

Evenings at home in the 1840s.

97

When every packet carried a reassurance!

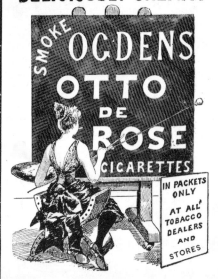

DELICIOUSLY CREAMY

SMOKE OGDENS OTTO DE ROSE CIGARETTES

IN PACKETS ONLY AT ALL TOBACCO DEALERS AND STORES

# CHOLERA.

## IMPORTANT DISCOVERY

BY

## DR. TASSINARI.

Dr. Tassinari has carried out a series of experiments with tobacco smoke upon the germs of various infectious disorders, with results which are satisfactory.

Smoke passed through a hollow ball containing Cholera bacilli had a fatal effect upon germ life.

## OGDEN'S OTTO DE ROSE CIGARETTES,

PURE VIRGINIA,

FIRST QUALITY,

PURE RICE PAPER,

## ARE UNRIVALLED.

Bloomer girls of the 1890s engaged in the new 'fast' pastime of cycling with its attendant hazards, one of the worst being 'collapsed eyeballs'!

98

A horseless carriage for two daring ladies of 1895.

*Home Chat* stuck to safer issues. In the fashion world, 'Camilla' and 'Lady Betty' laboured to sustain the illusion of their readers being part of a never-never-land, top-drawer scene. 'The exodus has commenced in very earnest, and London has become a barren plain in the wilderness . . . a desolate spot that Camilla and I are doomed to inhabit for a few days longer.' (*Home Chat*, 12 August 1905.)

Happily the wilderness was not without its oasis. 'As we remarked the other day at lunch at the Carlton, elbow sleeves are positively ubiquitous with the fete or reception gown. . . .'

'Margate, Ramsgate and Yarmouth have an average of 200,000 visitors in the course of a single season', they told readers. Lady Betty and Camilla were, of course, at hand with advice on 'the latest' in bathing costumes and 'the fancy . . . now prevailing of wearing stockings when swimming. Camilla says that once you have grown accustomed to the clinging sensations, stockings add materially to the clothed appearance of the wearer. The knickers finish . . . just short of the knee. Serge, wears splendidly—its one drawback being it is apt to chafe delicate skin. Scarlet bunting makes delightful swimming gowns. Another material in favour is bed-ticking. For a bathing dress you need $7\frac{1}{2}$ yards of 27 inch material.'

But holidays were not without pitfalls. 'Why', they asked, 'are so many girls today fagged and sallow . . . with lines about their eyes and mouths, and tired discontented expressions?' It was all due to the 'modern craze for speed' because they 'tax their powers beyond breaking point. Lie in a hammock in the orchard', they advise 'and leave your reading for a few days.' A reasonable suggestion if you lived, for instance in Endcliffe Vale Road, Sheffield, a district 'broken up by lovely pleasure houses, trees, shrubs, well-wooded parks. . . . Here and there you catch a glimpse of a spacious conservatory, or handsome stables . . . wealth flaunting its glories all around. . . .'

It was not so helpful if you lived in Sheffield's West Bar Green. 'From where we

stand, a narrow street rises so steeply it displays its garbage-littered road, paved with atrocious stones, strewn with ragged children, its two long lines of sordid houses. . . . All the property is old, squalid and black with the accumulated soot of generations. One street is swarming with rats. A dozen youngsters, barefooted and clad in nothing but ragged knickerbockers and old shirts, are walking in puddles.'

The necessarily abbreviated descriptions are from *The Penny Magazine* whose factual reporting, as contrasted with the Ruritanian comic-opera world of *Home Notes*, indicates the human misery and exploitation upon which the industrial 'prosperity' and opulence was founded.

'The female chainmaker . . . has to work with her child at her breast, or with a sharp eye on the little one as it crawls among the spark-sprinkled floor. Her hands blistered, or her body scorched with flying irons, she toils twelve hours a day, earns from 5s. to 8s. a week. The bellow-blowers, both children and old men and women, are worse paid . . . at the rate of 3d. per day, making a substantial profit for the owners who do not scruple to charge heavily for the fuel indispensable to the chainmakers.'

In an article 'Field Work for Women' from *Woman's World*, 1898, the writer rhapsodises: 'It is strange that any idea of degradation in field work should have arisen. It is the most poetic form of labour. A line of women, hoeing on a flat expanse

They all liked to stroll along the prom-prom-prom . . . (A Randolph Caldecott illustration.)

101

# WINCARNIS

## THE WORLD'S GREAT RESTORATIVE
## BRINGS THE ROSES BACK.

"Wincarnis" has been called the "Sunshine of Health," because it brings new life and new energy to the jaded body, just as the sunshine brings health to everything living. If you feel that Winter has depleted your health, and the Spring weather makes you languid and out of sorts, there is nothing that will pick you up and restore you like "Wincarnis." A well-known writer says : Town life makes terrific demands upon us, eats up our vitality, absorbs our reserve of physical force. Especially is this the case with women ; it does its best to break up the physical side of a woman's life. The débutante has a Season of wonderful successes frequently culminating in a brilliant marriage. Her cheeks are like a damask rose—but not for long, whispers the satirical *town*. It is too true ; the dainty blush gives way to a pallor almost transparent, the dimpled face loses its roundness, the buoyant step lags sadly through the carpeted room. A brilliant Season has collected the rates, and the beautiful fresh rose has faded. And yet, all these troubles might have been avoided. The glorious Season might have extended into many. The cheeks would have retained their pristine freshness, and the roundness would still be there. The rose would have been even rosier. "Wincarnis" would have done it all. It seems to the writer that it should be found in every household and in every boudoir.

## SEND FOR A FREE TRIAL BOTTLE.

### Travellers, Tourists, and Cyclists

should take "Wincarnis" on their journeys. It is most refreshing and sustaining. Shilling flasks are now sold by most licensed houses. They fit the pocket easily. If unable to get one in your district, send P.O. for 1s. direct to us. Refuse substitutes.

### SIGN THIS COUPON TO-DAY.

To COLEMAN & CO., Ltd. (315) Wincarnis Works, Norwich.

Please send me a Free Sample Bottle of "Wincarnis." I enclose 3d. to defray cost of carriage.

NAME .................................

ADDRESS ..............................

"Illustrated London News," May 11, 1911.

### AFTER FREE TRIAL

you can get "Wincarnis" from any Wine Merchant, Licensed Chemist or Grocer. It is also sold by the glass and in 1s. flasks at most hotels, high-class licensed houses, and at railway station refreshment-rooms. "Wincarnis" is also sold with quinine, or iron, or pepsine, or celery, all of which are beneficial in suitable cases.

---

The 'health wine' that sustained members of the House of Lords, House of Commons, debutantes, tourists and cyclists. Lyrical copywriting from *Home Chat* 1905. (Photograph by Jane Bridgeman.)

of sky . . . has a great nobility and beauty. The peasant who has done hard work in the fields . . . has the form a duchess might envy. To be wet through with the clean, wholesome rain is better than to be soaked in the sweat of stifling machine-sheds. To educate them . . . is worse than folly.'

For those on the hoe-ing end, the poetry, nobility and beauty were less obvious. The *Penny Magazine* records: 'On one farm I found women sleeping in a shed which had no windows . . . old sacks had to be hung up to exclude rain and wind. Men and women were huddled together . . . not that sleep was possible with so many people in a confined space. There was no place for the workers to dry their clothes, when, as often was the case, they had been gathering potatoes in the pouring rain all day.

'In another farm . . . workers rose at 4 a.m., had breakfast at 5 a.m. Gathering was very hard work . . . much too heavy, in my opinion for women. At 11.30 dinner, onions, ham and tea. We worked from then onwards to 6.30 p.m. without a break. Never again will I eat a potato without thinking of what back-breaking work it entails. . . . In Northumberland "eiderdowns" and "blankets" consisted of old sacks. . . . Go where you will . . . you will find women engaged in the . . . heaviest of

This establishment ensured, in 1899, that mourning 'became' not only Electra but also all its Victorian clientele.

field labour, with bare breasts, and sweating, tired faces.'

Lady Betty and Camilla's assertion in *Home Notes* that London 'had become deserted' must have been news to its shop assistants. To quote again from *The Penny Magazine* (1905): 'The shopgirl has her being between two fires. A fastidious and heartless public . . . and an exacting and ungenerous employer, aided often by a coarse and churlish shopwalker.

'Thousands of shopgirls would give five years of their lives to . . . say what they think of those who spend an idle afternoon . . . hunting the unfortunate assistant . . . taxing her physical strength by making her drag down box after box, without any intention of making a purchase.

'Fines of 3d. are imposed for "not showing goods willingly" for "failing to address the customer as Sir, or Madam" . . . or 2s. 6d. for allowing her to go without being spoken to.

'Hours range from sixty a week in the best shops, to 100 hours in smaller shops, with half an hour for dinner, and a quarter of an hour for tea, on the premises.

'The long standing, close atmosphere, short time for meals, care to keep things in their right place, and to make out accounts correctly; the long evenings with gaslight, and the liability to dismissal without warning, all tend to render the occupation of shop assistant trying . . . and injurious to health.'

Royal babies bawled for it . . . an ad from *The Young Mother's Magazine,* *c.* 1900. By courtesy of Mr Jack Hampshire, Baby Carriage Collection, Biddenden, Kent.

# ROYAL MOTHERS
### USE
# ASHTON & PARSONS' INFANTS' POWDERS

**For the little Princes and Princesses during the time of teething, and for fretfulness, and the many little ailments incident to infancy.**

THOUSANDS of Mothers testify to their worth, and their words are endorsed by Clergymen, Missionaries, Doctors, Nurses and Dealers from all parts of the world.

All who use Ashton & Parsons' Infants' Powders speak in the same high terms, and the more they are employed the more they are praised, as will be seen by the testimony of those who have on different occasions made extensive use of the Powders.

They cool the gums, comfort the child, produce a natural, calm, refreshing sleep, and render teething quite easy.

The Powders are guaranteed to be perfectly harmless, and so mild and gentle in their action that they may be given to any babe however young or delicate.

Their marvellous properties in relieving and preventing pain and disorder during the process of teething and the first few years of infant life are so extraordinary that, in many instances, they have been described by grateful mothers as being almost miraculous.

The Powders are pleasant to the taste and baby likes them, and they may be administered with the comforting knowledge that we guarantee them to be perfectly harmless.

On the following pages are a few of thousands of unsolicited Testimonials in praise of this absolutely safe and marvellous Infants' preservative.

## USED IN THE ROYAL NURSERIES.

ASHTON & PARSONS' INFANTS' POWDERS have been supplied by command to—

H.I.M. THE DOWAGER EMPRESS OF RUSSIA.
H.R.H. THE DUCHESS OF FIFE.
H.R.H. THE CROWN PRINCESS OF ROUMANIA.
H.I.H. THE GRAND DUCHESS OLGA OF RUSSIA.
H.R.H. PRINCE CAROL OF ROUMANIA.
H.R.H. PRINCESS ALEXANDER HOHENLOHE.
H.R.H. PRINCESS ELIZABETH OF ROUMANIA.
H.S.H. THE HEREDITARY PRINCESS OF LEININGEN.

And other Royal and distinguished personages, a unique example of their world-wide reputation and unparalleled excellence.

THEY ARE GUARANTEED TO BE PERFECTLY HARMLESS.

104

Nor did Lady Betty or Camilla so much as hint at the background of the fashion scene over which they presided so euphorically. To quote again from *The Penny Magazine* (1905), 'When a society function is to take place, the girls are driven like slaves. Some work for fifteen consecutive hours. In the coldest weather . . . workshops were without fires, the girls sitting in a temperature of 40 degrees.

'The mother of one young girl said her daughter arrived home . . . crying with exhaustion about 10.45 on Saturday nights. Young girls were found with faces careworn and sad before they were women, employed till midnight every Saturday and from 9.30 till 1 p.m. on Sunday mornings. One lady Inspector says "Nowhere have I seen such overcrowding . . . dirty ceilings and walls . . . workers so afraid of their employers. The dressmaker never gets her head up, she is continually under the eye of the forewoman . . . there is probably no class of workroom in which more vitiated air is breathed." '

What sense of shame or conscience the Edwardians possessed seemed occasioned not by such conditions, but by a failure to 'keep up with the Joneses'. 'She welcomed us . . . fastening her sleeves without apology. She brought in tea herself, and served it with an absence of shame at the freak of fortune which brought her so low as to be doing her own washing!' (*Woman's World*.)

Or there was the horror of not doing the 'done' thing: 'There has been much discussion as to whether asparagus should be picked off the plate between the thumb and first finger . . . but now tongs are sometimes supplied.' (*Home Notes*.)

The correct procedure to adopt in using visiting cards depended on quite a bewildering variety of contingencies, as the *Penny Magazine* of 1905 pointed out:

'The leaving of visiting cards is a matter that needs far more knowledge and consideration than one would at first thought imagine; that is . . . if the custom is to be conducted decently.

'A married lady when calling upon a married couple leaves two of her husband's cards, and one of her own; in the case of a widow she leaves but one; but if her call be upon a single lady she only leaves her own card, since it is not strict etiquette for a gentleman to leave his card on a spinster.

'Callers wishing to leave their cards upon the hall table, should do so when leaving, not entering.

'When the corner of a card is turned down it may imply two things; it denotes that the visitor has called in person, or on the other hand, that the whole family has called.

'With regard to the new institution of sending cards by post, the method should never be resorted to after an entertainment; the card must always be left in person; but cards to inquire after a sick friend or acquaintance may be sent by a servant.

'After an entertainment a card should be left within a week; after a dinner party or ball it is not sufficient to leave a card only, but the lady of the house must be asked for. After weddings and "tea fights" it is permissible to leave cards upon the way out, so as to avoid calling later on. After a garden party there is no occasion to call; this is the one exception.

An advertisement that epitomised the patent medicine boom, from *Weldon's Illustrated Dressmaker*, 1902. By courtesy of Warwick Museum Services.

Opposite. Ads solved every problem – from wash-day blues to fits, red noses to old false teeth. *Home Chat*, 1905.

# They Kept Us Well

## for

# 14

## Years.

Mrs. M. A. Tolhurst.

On October 1st, 1900, Mrs. M. A. Tolhurst, of 18, Park Street, Ashford, Kent, said :—" I have been through torture with pains in the back, urinary discomfort, and dropsical swellings, resulting from a weakness of the kidneys.

"My illness kept me to my bed for days together, in fact, quite crippled me at times so that I dared not stoop or even turn in bed. It caused constant headache, languor and depression, and a bloodshot condition of the eyeballs that gave me great anxiety about my sight.

"In spite of expensive medical treatment I became worse and worse, and do not know how matters would have gone had I not turned at last to Doan's Backache Kidney Pills.

"Within a week of starting with Doan's Pills my health improved considerably, and I eagerly continued the treatment. Its effect has been a revelation to all who know me, for I am now completely cured of every sign of kidney or bladder weakness, and am fit and well again in body, limbs, and eyesight. I have only Doan's Pills to thank for my splendid cure.

(Signed) "M. A. Tolhurst."

On May 26th, 1914, Mrs. Tolhurst says :—" Owing to the interest aroused by my case I want it placed on record that Doan's Pills effected such a thorough cure that it has lasted 14 years, and I am still as well as ever."

## Why? *Because*

Doan's Backache Kidney Pills which Mrs. Tolhurst and Mr. Stephenson praise and recommend so highly, are just exactly what they claim to be, a special and efficient kidney medicine.

They have a direct strengthening, healing and curative action solely upon the kidneys and bladder, by which direct means they prevent, relieve and often permanently cure the disorders which are due to kidney complaint, such as:—

## Backache, Rheumatism, Dropsy, Inflamed Bladder, Blood Diseases, Sciatica, Lumbago, Stone, Gravel, Urinary Weaknesses,

### And other Uric-Acid Ailments.

It is the thoroughness of their cures that has gained for Doan's Pills the world-wide reputation they enjoy.

Price 2/9 a box, 6 boxes 13/9. FOSTER-McCLELLAN Co., 8, Wells Street, Oxford Street, London, W. ; also at Cape Town, S.A ; Sydney, N.S.W. ; Shanghai, China ; and Buffalo, N.Y.

Mr. W. Stephenson.

On February 2nd, 1900, Mr. W. Stephenson, of 19, Murchison Street, Scarborough, said :—

"For twenty-five years I have had kidney complaint, and suffered agony from pains in my back and loins. Their suddenness would take my breath away, and I got to dread the very thought of it. The trouble seemed incurable, for one symptom or another distressed me always. If the weather was damp I had rheumatism in the arms and legs, and at other times violent headaches, bladder trouble, and dizziness.

"I got in such a state that I was afraid of walking any distance for fear of falling.

"But one day, when feeling at my worst, I bought a box of Doan's Pills. The first few doses made a change in me, and I continued the treatment until after three boxes of this medicine I can truthfully say that every symptom of kidney complaint has left my system. I am better now in health than ever I remember.

"I make this statement out of gratitude for all Doan's Pills have done for me, and hope to be the means of helping other kidney sufferers.

(Signed) "W. Stephenson."

Fourteen years later, Mr. Stephenson says:—" There has never been the slightest return of my old complaint since Doan's Backache Kidney Pills cured me fourteen years ago. I am well over 60 now, and am still enjoying the splendid health they brought me."

# Doan's Pills.

DOAN'S BACKACHE KIDNEY PILLS
TRADE MARK

'Always remember to return a first call within a week, whether you may desire or not to cultivate the acquaintance. Should there be any reason for your not wishing to know the new callers, you may leave your cards . . . without asking for the lady of the house.'

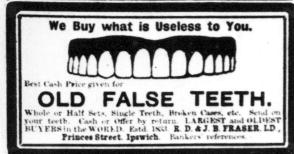
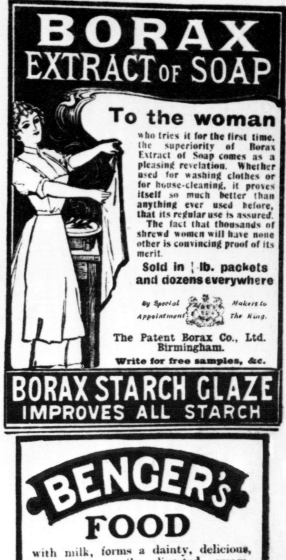
Fiction-wise the moustache twirlers were still hard at it. 'She noticed his eyes were fixed upon her ... and that his nervous habit of twirling his moustache was beginning to assert itself.'

'With blazing eyes Lady Tracey turned upon her nephew. "How dare they accuse

Queue for
carriages.
Debutantes of
1904 after
presentation at
court.

me of murdering my husband! I am wholly innocent!" Henry gazed at her . . . and
began thoughtfully to twirl his moustache.'

Wealth could prove as great an impediment to 'true love' as poverty, for these
ingenuous heroines. 'He believed her to be a badly paid companion. Would he mind
that she had almost more money than she knew what to do with?' Possibly not—if
the cash was inherited. Trade begotten 'filthy lucre' was another matter. The hero of
a *Mother and Home* story (1913), confides to his best friend: 'Her father made a good
income at some trade. She's an awfully nice girl, but she's got "trade" stamped on
every line of her adorable body.' Despite this unspeakable deformity, he marries her,
albeit not without misgivings. 'As Forsyth walked up the aisle, he noticed on one
side sat the representatives of the world professional, and upon the other the fat,
comfortable men of business, their wives and daughters.'

Class distinction with its all-embracing, claustrophobic tentacles extended even as
far as the postal service. '*How about the Queen's private letters? Is it possible they are jostled
with vulgar familiarity by tradesmen's bills, and mispelt half-penny postcards, in one common
bag?*' (*Home Notes.*)

Drink continued to be a problem from which even 'lady typewriters' were not
immune. 'An authority on the matter, Dr T. Olwen, affirms that lady typewriters
make more mistakes when taking alcohol.' This may have accounted for the
'inadvertent errors' beloved of business jargon. Or were these caused by 'three

o'clock fatigue'? For according to a small ad, 'Monarch typewriters save the operator from three o'clock fatigue, and ensure the last hour's work is equal to the first.'

The effects of stooping over a hot typewriter all day could be counteracted by 'Dolabel shoulder braces, indispensable to ladies who sit much. Price 4s. 6d. post free.'

The nation's health, or lack of it, was reflected in the overwhelming preponderance of patent-medicine ads. So-called 'cures' provided a bonanza for quacks and reputable medical men alike. As H. G. Wells's novel *Tono-Bungay* witnesses, it was the hey-day of the patent-medicine manufacturer. Nor was there any Trades Descriptions Act to inhibit claims such as: *'Consumption can be cured!* At last a remedy . . . that cures consumption . . . even in the advanced stages of the disease . . . after all other remedies had failed.'

'Unsolicited testimonials' abounded likewise: '. . . my husband had for many years had severe inflamation of the lungs . . . all feared he would die. . . . After taking your medicine he was never ill afterwards.' Somewhat ambiguously the 'reference' ends: 'The Rev. G. W. Hope, our late Minister, has corresponded with you for me, for several years. I find it do me good whenever I get a cold.'

'Cures' abounded, for blushing to bronchitis, asthma to anaemia, rickets to rheumatism, deafness to dropsy, nerves to neuritis, dyspepsia to diphtheria, hysteria to hiccoughs, fits to fatigue, indigestion to impetigo, infantile ailments to influenza, 'women's ailments' to worms, perspiration to 'premature decay', brain-fag to boils.

Red noses could be 'permanently restored to their natural colour'. Remedies for bad breath came 'secretly packed'. And Ruritania breaks through, astonishingly, in a testimonial from no less a personage than Her Imperial Highness, Empress of All the Russias, bestowing her Gracious Patronage on Neaves Food for Nerves. Poor lady, she was soon to need it.

Even the realistic *Penny Magazine* was not above writing a glowing 'puff' for Mother Seigal's Syrup. 'Never before have doctors rejected so many of our young men as unfit for military service. . . . The cause is not far to seek. The strain . . . in modern life has made us a nation of dyspeptics. Except when aided by Mother Seigal's Syrup, how few of us digest food naturally and easily, converting it into rich, pure blood.' Mother Seigal's Syrup was also a 'proven remedy' for 'stomach disorders, rheumatism, brain-fag, impoverished blood, nervous headaches, sleeplessness, neuralgia, mental exhaustion, influenza, hysteria'.

Elsewhere, a glum-looking old gentleman, 'formerly as deaf as a post' testified that he could 'now hear the mantel clock ticking from eight yards away'.

Those who deplore our modern dependence on tranquillisers might find it instructive to ponder on our forebears' obsession with 'nerves'. That epilepsy was commonplace seems proven both by the idiomatic phrase 'having a fit' and the plethora of alleged 'cures'—'for fits, hysteria and St Vitus Dance'.

High infant mortality rates sometimes produced 'cures' that were worse than the disease. 'Don't let your child die! Fennings children's powders do not contain

Railway
vandals of the
past. Article
from *Home
Chat*, 1905.
From author's
collection.
(Photograph
by Geoff
Mayor.)

August 5, 1905. **HOME CHAT.** 327

near a farmhouse, so that one can get a supply of milk and fresh eggs for breakfast in the morning. Also, if the weather is cold, one may want to borrow one or two blankets, which can always be done for a trifling consideration. Pitch the tent behind a hedge, or in some position where it is sheltered from the wind, and if possible camp near a river, canal, or pond where a good supply of fresh water may be had. Avoid camping near the high road, or by a footpath, as there one is liable to attract too much attention for comfort, and to meet with tramps, gipsies, and other undesirable persons.

# RAILWAY CARRIAGE WRECKERS.

**The Old-fashioned Foot-Warmer was not an Easy Thing to Steal, but One Company lost 700 in a Short While. Glasses, Decanters, Soap and Towels also Disappear, and Carriage Fittings are Cut and Hacked.**

FRAUDULENT railway passengers, who have been discovered and forced to pay, after trying to travel free, often vent their spite on the company by throwing floor-mats out of window, tearing down the blinds, or doing other wilful damage to the compartment in which they are travelling.

A Whitechapel racing man was caught the other day by one of the ever-vigilant examiners at Vauxhall giving up a ticket from Wimbledon, although the train he was in had not stopped at that station.

As it seemed clear to the officials that the "sportsman" had travelled up from Salisbury, the latter deemed discretion the better part of valour, and reluctantly disgorged, swearing, however, to "get his own back" from the company. Unknown to him, a smart examiner slipped into the next compartment and travelled with the train to Waterloo, where an examination showed that the racing man and his pals had got their money's worth out of the company by cutting off the window-straps, tearing down the netting of the luggage-racks, and slashing up the cushions of the carriage.

Three of the men were sent to gaol, and a fourth was fined for assaulting one of the company's servants.

In this instance the cutting off of the window-straps was an act of revenge, a motive absent in the case of a third-rate actor convicted recently of cutting leather straps from the windows of L.B. & S.C.R. carriages.

### The Cobbler and the Straps.

The mummer pleaded that some time before a professional friend of his had recommended railway-carriage window-straps as excellent razor-strops! He had tried one, and was so delighted with the result that he wished to make presents to his friends. A Wandsworth cobbler, when prosecuted for the same offence, admitted using leather window-straps for soleing children's shoes!

Up-to-date companies, like the L. & S.-W.R., years ago provided large numbers of lavatory carriages on all long-distance trains.

The travelling public immediately showed its appreciation of the boon. So did railway-carriage thieves—by annexing water-decanters, glasses, toilet-paper, and towels in ever-increasing quantity.

On a Birmingham man's house being searched, a large wooden linen-chest in the kitchen was found to contain 186 towels, bearing the monogram or initials of the L. & N.-W.R., the Midland Railway, the G.N.R., and several North British lines.

Quite recently an eight-year-old lad was arrested by a Manchester policeman for hawking in the streets rolls of toilet-paper actually branded with the initials of various railway companies! These he had abstracted at night-time from lavatory carriages while lying unprotected in the sidings.

Foot-warmers are regarded by most railway companies as relics of a bygone age.

### The Disappearing Foot-warmers.

But the South-Eastern and Chatham line clings to its comforts of long ago.

Possibly as a protest against such conservatism, certain persons recently determined to annex as many S.E. & C.R. foot-warmers as they could lay their hands on; and for weeks on end the company lost one or two "warmers" a day, until the number missing totalled over 700.

A few weeks ago a man was sentenced to a month's hard labour at the Guildhall Police Court for being in possession of a S.E. & C.R. foot-warmer, alleged to be of the extraordinary value of fifteen shillings.

In the old "foot-warmer days," before the present reign of hot-air heating on the L. & S.-W.R. this popular line experienced great trouble with its sailor passengers, who loved to "launch" foot-warmers from the carriage windows while travelling at fifty or sixty miles an hour.

According to an official of the S.E. & C.R., there has recently been a remarkable falling off in the number of insulting messages scribbled by irate passengers on the walls and ceiling of the company's carriages.

calomel, opium, morphia or anything injurious to the tender babe.'

In the cosmetic field, 'beautiful complexions' were 'guaranteed' by Pomeroy Skin Food. 'Oatine powder leaves' were 'the latest toilet acquisition'. Mr Eugen Sandow, the 'strong man', was at hand with advice on how to make 'Men out of Men, and Women out of Women'.

Bungalows sold at £200, built to order £250, and 'completely furnished' for an extra 45 guineas. The magic words 'payments deferred' made their appearance. The Hackney Furnishing Co. Ltd. offered a wardrobe, dressing-table, chest of drawers and mirror, chair, and towel-holder for £5.15.0. or 23 monthly payments of 5s. each. 'No deposit required. Free Life Insurance and Free Fire Insurance.' Patrons were told, 'for the convenience of customers arriving by train . . . our private brougham will be sent, conveying visitors to the showrooms and back, free of charge. Luncheon provided. Customers visiting . . . from the country are allowed full railway fares on orders from £30 upwards.'

A realistic approach to the everyday problems of ordinary women inspired *Woman's Weekly* which made its appearance on 4 November 1911. The claim of its first editor, Miss 'Biddy' Johnson, that 'the dominant note throughout is usefulness' still stands. 'Our desire is to please the average woman.' Its contents consisted of a gentle mix of embroidery and knitting patterns, cookery recipes, hints on baby-care, fiction and practical fashion.

'Last winter we were held in thraldom by the hobble-skirt, and were actually threatened with trousers. . . . The hobble skirt made itself obnoxious to the makers of under petticoats who lost trade by it, and was the cause of so many accidents that the best dressmakers resolved to "kill" it.'

Fiction followed the conventional pattern. In 'The Girl who Lost her Beauty' the heroine, whose face was disfigured by scalding, meets her betrothed after three years' absence, and wonders, 'Will he love me now?'

'A sob rose from her throat . . . a wild, despairing sob, for she thought he was too shocked to speak. She choked back the sob, and the head which had been held so proudly, dropped.'

# CHAPTER EIGHT

# *War and Peace*

IN 1887 Dame Millicent Garrett Fawcett (1847–1929) became spokesman for the Women's Suffrage Movement. By 1903 Emmeline Pankhurst organised the Woman's Social and Political Union of Women Suffragettes, and 8 March 1914 saw the publication of their weekly journal, the *Women's Dreadnought*. 'The name of our paper is symbolic of the fact that the women who are fighting for freedom must fear nothing.'

It was no empty boast. The malicious ridicule to which Women's Lib is subjected today, is a pale shadow of the almost incredible male hysteria which greeted the Women's Suffrage Movement.

'Presently, to my surprise, the whole mass of blackness surged towards me. I saw a small, elderly and feeble woman being torn to pieces near me . . . about twenty men pulling her one way, while as many were pulling her another.' (Description of an East London Federation meeting in Trafalgar Square, 21 March 1914.)

'Prison News. Miss Ethel Moorhead, who complained that whilst . . . being forcibly fed in Carlton Prison, her ear was burnt with hot irons, and that she was left at the mercy of young students from the asylum, and kept on the operating table for the whole of one day, is now gravely ill. Dr C. R. Cadell reports she is suffering from pneumonia as a result of the injection of some foreign substance into her lungs, and that the patient is suffering from extreme breathlessness and an enlarged heart.' (*The Dreadnought*, 28 March 1913.)

The paper also fearlessly exposed social and working conditions.

'*Sweated drudgery*. "I work from 8.30 a.m. to 8.30 at night. I am a general ironer, and on one day, for ironing 72 pieces, one coat and a dress, I earned 2s. 3d." This woman has to keep herself and a delicate girl of ten.' (28 March 1913.)

'Refusing to accept reductions in their pay . . . to about 25 per cent off their wages, 100 women and a few men employed by a hosiery manufacturer of Sawley Gate, Leicester, have been locked out. A notice has been posted at the factory gates that only non-Unionists will be employed.'

'*Hungry children*: In the week ending 20 March 1914, 4,986 children went so hungry to school that the London County Council Care Committee was obliged to provide them with food. Most of the children . . . had nothing to eat but that one school meal a day.'

*Britannia*, a campaigning penny weekly which ran from 9 October 1915 to 30 December 1918, was edited by Sylvia and Christabel Pankhurst, and assisted,

Left. The youthful newly-crowned Queen Victoria
provided an attractive inner-cover picture for the 1 July
1838 edition of *World of Fashion*. By courtesy of Warwick
Museum Services. (Photograph by Geoff Mayor.)

Right. Downing Street was the scene of this suffragette
protest in 1908.
Above. 'Sweet girl graduates' – an innovation in the
world of learning. Cambridge graduates of the 1890s.

A typical
periodical of
the 1890s, its
cover
illustration
(though later
to be
lampooned)
equally typical
of existing
conditions. By
courtesy of
Warwick
Records
Office.
(Photograph
by Geoff
Mayor.)

# THE BRITISH WORKWOMAN.

EIGHTEEN YEARS AGO.—"At last she stood, half wild with hunger and anguish."—*See page 75*.

# WOOLLAND BROTHERS.
## Motoring & Country Hats in exclusive designs.

**"Charlotte Corday" Bonnet,** for Motoring, in fine Tegal,
edged with a pleating of narrow Ribbon, trimmed with large Choux
and Strings of Soft Ribbon and Chiffon Veil to tone, in pretty
quaint combinations of Colourings.   Price **49/6.**

## 95, 97, 99, 101, 103, 105, & 107, KNIGHTSBRIDGE, LONDON, S.W.

Early morning required protection from dusty roads, wind and rain.

How to 'electrify' your personality with the aid of Harness' magnetic corsets.

Fishing for compliments . . . or what the smart young lady of fashion wore at the seaside. By courtesy of Leamington Spa Art Gallery. (Photograph by John Bridgeman.)

somewhat surprisingly, by the famous singer, Dame Clara Butt.

Linked in spirit with the largely middle- and upper-class dominated Women's Suffrage Movement, was the Women's Trade Union League. Their monthly magazine, *The Woman Worker* (1d.), the Journal of the Women's Trade Union, edited by Mary Macarthur, first appeared in August 1907. Its aim was to present 'the struggle for betterment, representing the women's side in a way never done before'. Words were followed by deeds when its editor backed the strike of the Midland women chain-makers. Robert Blatchford, editor of the Socialist journal, *The Clarion*

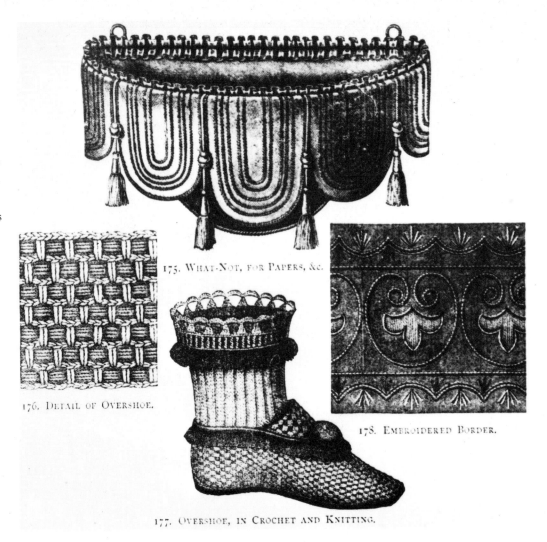

Examples of 'the trifles – utterly unworthy of their richness and strength, to which the finest faculties in the world' were confined, from *The Young Englishwoman*, 1871. Author's collection. (Photograph by Jane Bridgeman.)

175. WHAT-NOT, FOR PAPERS, &c.

176. DETAIL OF OVERSHOE.

178. EMBROIDERED BORDER.

177. OVERSHOE, IN CROCHET AND KNITTING.

(first published 1891) and the man responsible for converting Daisy, Countess of Warwick from an Edwardian socialite into a Socialist M.P., became a popular contributor.

Advertisements, such as the one published by the Felt Hatters and Trimmers Union, urged readers:

'Don't complain about hard conditions ... and then go out and without discrimination purchase your commodities. Buy Union Made Goods. Insist upon seeing the Union-made label under the leather. *No woman should tolerate a man who wears an unlabelled hat.*'

Petticoats rather than hats preoccupied *Vogue*'s editorial at its launching eight years later, on 15 September 1916.

'Paris openings made it indubitably clear that crinolines have taken French leave. One shudders to think what will become of the petticoat ... those airy ruffles, those

bewitching frills, to what fate will they be consigned?'

Two months previously the fate of 60,000 men killed and 73,000 men 'missing' had been 'consigned' at the battle of the Somme. The five-day bombardment preceding the attack was heard in London. The wounded and the dying congested London's railway stations. *Vogue* readers were prepared to make sacrifices.

'The late Summer is no longer London's close season. Whether from petrol shortage or patriotism, cars are few and far between. Taxis are as elusive as the bluebird. . . . So one goes by bus and finds the brightest and best of one's friends hanging, strap in hand, slightly self-conscious and uncertain of the formulae, but as pleased as a dog who has learned a new trick.'

War was not without its consolations, such as smart, unusual dress! 'Some friends are in smart nurse's uniforms, or in dashing uniforms with brass buttons.' There was also romance: 'The pleading of a son of Mars . . . is too much for some hero-worshipping daughter of Venus. Who cares if she has never seen him except in khaki? Or whether the pay of a Second Loot can be considered sufficient support for a wife and problematical soldier or two in 1936? For the moment, the romance of all ages is hers.'

*Vogue*'s superlative presentation, photography and subject-matter epitomised, as it still does, a dream world peopled by the rich, the beautiful, the famous. Its first issue offered fur coats at 35 guineas, suits at 8 gns, nightdresses at 39s. 6d. Staggering

Another popular monthly in 1898, posing a surprisingly modern query about journalism as a profession for women.

Annie S. Swans Magazine

# The Woman at Home

March 1898

No. 54  Price 6d.

THE
DUCHESSES
OF ENGLAND

With Many New and Rare
Portraits

By Mrs. F. HARCOURT WILLIAMSON

AMUSEMENTS
By IAN MACLAREN

THE FAIR AMERICAN
By ANNIE S. SWAN

SISTER NINA
By INA LEON CASSILIS

AND ALL THE

R. CROCKETT'S

HODDER AND
STOUGHTON

IS JOURNALISM
A GOOD PROFESSION
FOR WOMEN?

Symposium by
Mrs. JACK JOHNSON, Mrs. HUMPHRY,
W. ROBERTSON NICOLL, MARY FRANCES
BILLINGTON, Miss ELLA CURTIS

THE QUEEN'S VISITS TO
HER PRIME MINISTERS

With Numerous Portraits
and other Illustrations

THE EARLY SPRING
FASHIONS
By Mrs. ARIA

USUAL FEATURES

SERIAL STORY

27 Paternoster Row
LONDON E.C.

sums in the days when the average family man earned between 18s. and 25s. a week.

Small wonder that 'Lizzie in the basement' no longer entirely reconciled to 'the station in life in which it had pleased God (and her employers) to keep her', dreamed of 'becoming a lady'. A popular 'recitation piece' of the day recounts:

> I'm just a simple scullery maid,
> I'm what you'd call 'no class'

and relates her dreams of being wooed by 'a gent' who showers her with 'jewels, motor-cars and coronets of gold'. The ultimate accolade was marriage with the Prince of Wales (later the Duke of Windsor), the golden boy whose winning grin adorned every calendar and women's magazine in the land.

> His Highness was proposing once,
> 'Yus, Teddy dear', I says,
> When cook yells in the kitchen,
> 'Hi, Emma—orf to bed!'

Capitalising on the age-old appeal of the Cinderella syndrome, was the journal whose name became a household word — *Peg's Paper*. Unlikely as it sounds, it was conceived in a Wigan churchyard, the brain-child of Nell Kennedy, wife of F. J. Lamburn (right-hand man to Sir Arthur Pearson) and mother of I.P.C. Director, Miss Patricia Lamburn. Miss Lamburn recounts:

Left. What the fashionable woman was wearing in the 1890s, as depicted in *The Lady*, 3 May 1894. By courtesy of Warwick Museum Services. (Photograph by Geoff Mayor.)

Right. Milady's maid had every detail of her life and duties prescribed by strict etiquette.

Marylebone
Workhouse
interior
(1850–1915).
Victorian
charity fell
lamentably
short of its
pious
preachings.

'I don't know what prompted the concept of *Peg's Paper*, but she (Nell Kennedy) went to Wigan, the centre of cotton mills and local industry, and sat for six weeks every day listening to the conversation of the mill girls as they took their lunch break. The result was *Peg's Paper* . . . a sensitive and accurate reflection of what those girls wanted; emotional satisfaction, thrills, romance.'

The weeklies, *Glamour*, *Star*, *Lucky Star* and *Silver Star* were also launched by this remarkable young woman, together with *Novel Magazine* publishing such literary giants as H. G. Wells. But none achieved *Peg's Paper*'s million-plus sales.

Issue No. 1 of *Peg's Paper* ($1\frac{1}{2}$d. a week) appeared 15 May 1919, its opening article captioned 'Let's be Pals'. Covers, printed in black and red, illustrated the serial's highlight, captured and captioned with unerring skill by Nell Kennedy. Cover No. 1 depicted a mill girl accompanied by a slick-looking 'gent', while a

Charles Dickens decorates the cover of *The Queen*, 3 May 1862. By courtesy of *Harpers and The Queen*, National Magazine Co., London. (Photograph by Jane Bridgeman.)

A Kate
Greenaway
illustration for
*The Girl's Own
Annual*, 1896.

124

distraught mother exclaims: 'Oh Janet, he won't marry you!'—'An incident from our splendid story, "Was she a wife".' The serials, written by Nell Kennedy herself, proved compulsive reading. They bore provocative titles such as 'Parted by a kiss', 'She made him love her', 'The woman who came between'.

The mother's fears in story No. 1 that the rich man would not marry her daughter were, in fact, uncharacteristic. Not for these heroines the 'sinking into an early grave' or any of the afflictions of unrequited love suffered by their grandmothers. Like the Canadian mounties they 'got their man'—and to a hero they were rich, titled, handsome, bemedalled, usually demobbed V.C.s never below the rank of Captain. Their triumph was accompanied by a curious, inverted snobbery.

'I am only a factory girl', she said, 'but I was determined to make you love me.'

'She was only an embroideress in a smart dressmaker's establishment, but a rich man loved her.'

'I cared ——' she whispered in a stifled voice, 'but I am only a servant, and you ——.'

Heroines were unfailingly beautiful, usually with cornflower blue eyes and golden hair. Villians and villainesses were 'foreign', swarthy, brunette, 'sullen-eyed'.

Despite their being blue-eyed, blond-haired and upper-crust, *Peg's Paper*'s heroes proved anything but gentlemanly losers.

'You have spurned me and you shall pay for it!' they hiss. 'You have stolen my

All set to become beautiful belles: Victorian children's fashions. By courtesy of Leamington Spa Art Gallery. (Photograph by John Bridgeman.)

125

The youthful
Queen
Victoria and
Prince Albert,
engaged in
what *The Lady*
of 1885
described as 'a
dreadful
nightmare of a
waltz'. By
courtesy of
Leamington
Spa Art
Gallery.
(Photograph
by Geoff
Mayor.)

sweetheart but I shall be revenged!' An otherwise meek heroine warns her 'dark and
beautiful as the night' rival—'You have stolen by babies' name, but you shall pay
for this!' It is a matter of conjecture why 'revenge', so constant a theme in these and
earlier stories, should have virtually disappeared from modern fiction.

That new, magical form of entertainment, 'The Kinema', was also covered by a
feature, 'Peg trots around Filmland'. Issue No. 13 in 1919 quotes still redoubtable

THE TESTIMONY OF THE NIGHTINGALE, THE LILY, AND THE ROSE.

# PEARS' SOAP

"*It is matchless for the Hands and Complexion.*"

*Adelina Patti.*

Yᴱ NIGHTINGALE.

"*I prefer it to any other Soap.*"

*Lillie Langtry.*

Yᴱ LILY.

"*For preserving the complexion, it is the finest Soap in the world.*"

*Marie Roze.*

Yᴱ ROSE.

The Nightingale (Patti, the singer), the Lily (Lillie Langtry) and the Rose (Marie Roze, operatic singer) were all evidently inspired by Pears' soap.

127

# HOMOCEA
## Cures Chilblains

**For Chilblains, Chaps, Roughness, Red Noses, Coughs, and Colds in the Head, Homocea stands unrivalled as a universal and permanent cure and preventative. The scantiest application generally gives relief.**

" I was persuaded to use Homocea for Chilblains, to which I am a martyr after two applications the chilblains disappeared, though this severe weather is still with us as I write."   ETHEL COMYNS.

9, Arundel Street, Srand, London, W.C.

names such as Charlie Chaplin, Conrad Nagel, Douglas Fairbanks, Mary Pickford, William S. Hart and Billie Burke. It also relates how film-star Veleska Suratt 'once earned £1 a week in a milliner's shop. Today, £500 for the same period would not excite her. Her theatrical training was obtained through the kindness of the Grand Duke Boris of Russia who, meeting her at a dinner party asked her the greatest wish

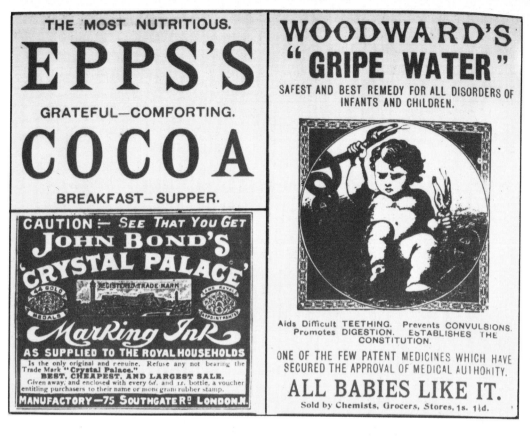

Some popular turn-of-the-century ads.

of her life. She told him: 'To be an actress.' Whereupon he wrote her a cheque for £400. Wasn't she lucky?'

And who are we to question how a £1-week shop assistant came to be at a dinner party with a Russian aristocrat, or to suspect this was only the children's version, if it warmed the heart of some overworked, underpaid 'skivvy', who blacking stoves with chilblained fingers at 6 a.m. on some freezing winter's morning, dreamed that she too might some day meet an obliging Russian Grand Duke with a cheque book at the ready?

History is also inadvertently recorded in *Peg's Paper* via an advertisement: 'Captain Sir John Alcock K.B.C., D.S.C. writes: "We [himself and co-pilot A.W. Brown] found Fry's chocolate wonderfully sustaining in our flight across the Atlantic. . . . It was our chief, solid food." ' This first-ever Atlantic flight (14–15 June 1919) earned Alcock and Brown knighthoods and the *Daily Mail* prize of £10,000. Sir John Alcock was killed on 18 December of that year on a flight between London and Paris.

Gaining readers 'upstairs' as fast as *Peg's Paper* 'downstairs' was *Homes and Gardens*, first published in 1919 and still flourishing. Its initial issue, describing a bedroom 'with a hanging cord for ringing a bell in the servant's bedroom' retained a distinctly Victorian ambience. But the shorter hours and higher pay offered by

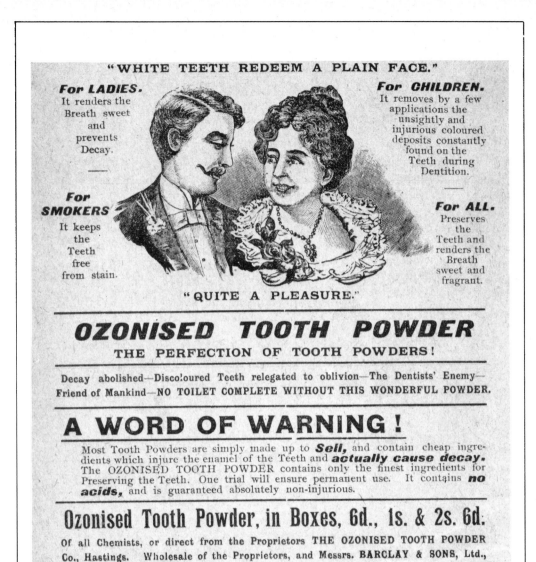

Ozonised tooth powder offered hope, even to the plain. By courtesy of Erica Pulbrook.

factories, as well as widening opportunities for women, made those 'summoned by bells' a fast-diminishing race. So while Ruritania and Romance flourished in the basement, Madam in the drawing room earnestly pursued those 'features of a practical nature' promised in *Homes and Gardens'* opening editorial. For women reared on the gospel that 'a lady's hands must always be white and soft' it was a traumatic experience. The recurring phrase, 'the servantless home', assumed a pathos second only to that of 'a motherless child'. Erudite sociologists, historians and art-historians, assessing the twenties' 'aesthetic revolt against Victorianism' are

Cadbury's
Cocoa,
'untouched by
human hand',
lent stamina to
penny-farthing
cyclists.

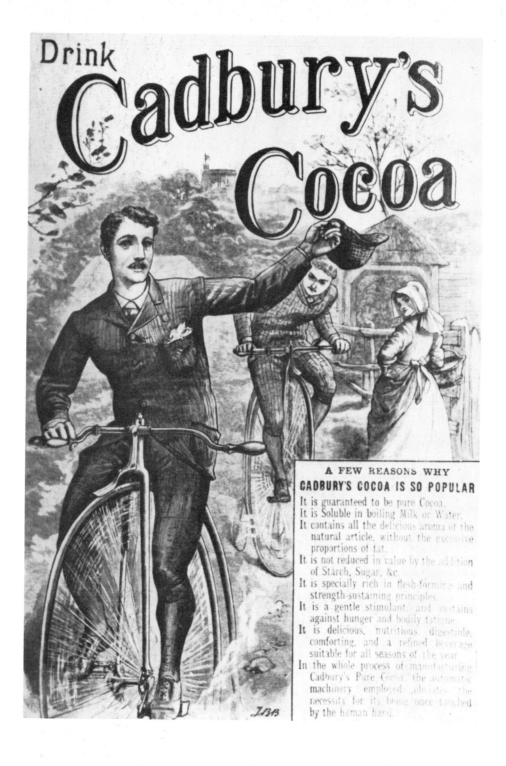

Drink Cadbury's Cocoa

A FEW REASONS WHY

**CADBURY'S COCOA IS SO POPULAR**

It is guaranteed to be pure Cocoa.

It is Soluble in boiling Milk or Water.

It contains all the delicious aroma of the natural article, without the excessive proportions of fat.

It is not reduced in value by the addition of Starch, Sugar, &c.

It is specially rich in flesh-forming and strength-sustaining principles.

It is a gentle stimulant, and sustains against hunger and bodily fatigue.

It is delicious, nutritious, digestible, comforting, and a refined beverage suitable for all seasons of the year.

In the whole process of manufacturing Cadbury's Pure Cocoa the automatic machinery employed obviates the necessity for its being once touched by the human hand.

"The Subjects Best Friend"

# HUDSON'S DrySoap

Home & Clothes as Sweet as a Rose

Queen Victoria, complete with Albert medallion, somewhat incongruously championing Hudson's Dry Soap.

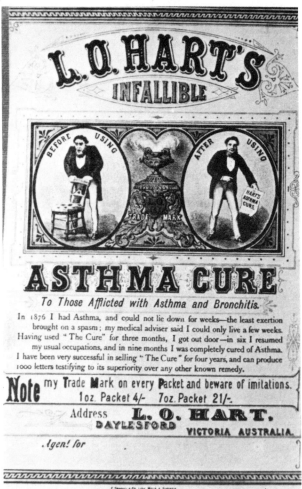

apt to overlook the obvious. If the average middle-class woman developed a sudden passion for 'aesthetically' bare walls, uncluttered spaces, discarded once-precious bric-a-brac by the sackful, she was motivated not by any blinding flash of 'aesthetic awareness', but by the hideous realisation that if all that junk was to be dusted, cleaned and polished, she herself would have to do it. A prize-winning essay on 'A house without a servant' advised that pictures be removed from walls, ornaments packed away, brass painted black, coal-fires replaced by gas-fires. Kitchen tables covered with linoleum would not need scrubbing. Tea trolleys dispensed with table-laying, old fashioned knives could be replaced by the new stainless steel, brass stair-rods with brackets.

'Is polished brass worthwhile?' was the burning question in the servantless home. Other articles in an 'intrepid pioneer' spirit discuss 'My experiences with an anthracite stove' 'The floor I painted', and 'How shall I treat my stairs?'

Even the erstwhile socially-conscious *Penny Magazine* complained: 'The servant

134

THE

LADIES' TREASURY

FOR 1887.

A HOUSEHOLD MAGAZINE.

EDITED BY

MRS. WARREN.

———

ILLUSTRATED.

———

LONDON:
BEMROSE AND SONS,
23, OLD BAILEY.

Title page of *The Ladies' Treasury*. This Mrs Warren's profession was quite unlike that of the lady of the same name in Shaw's famous play. In 1887 Shaw was thirty-one, living at home with his mother who may, perhaps, have subscribed to this journal. By courtesy of Miss Kate Fryer, Birmingham.

*Hearth and Home*, a giant-sized women's monthly, was first published in 1891. Edited by the 'notorious' Frank Harris, it was designed for the more educated, less romantically orientated woman. By courtesy of Warwick Museum Services (Photograph by Geoff Mayor.)

136

Love plus Enòs Health Salts was a sure recipe for a happy marriage according to this Victorian ad.

Fashionable
wear for the
Coronation of
George V and
Queen Mary.
By courtesy of
Warwick
Museum
Services.
(Photograph
by Geoff
Mayor.)

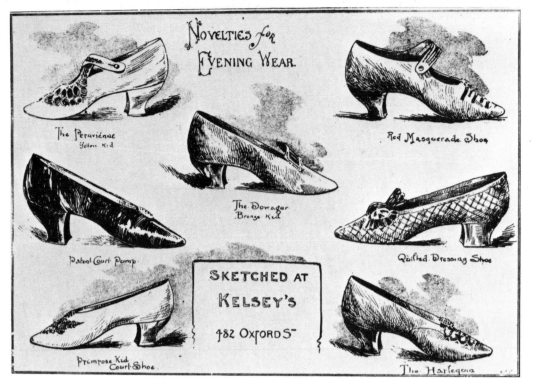

The latest in evening foot-wear as shown in *The Lady*, 19 Nov. 1891. By courtesy of Warwick Museum Services. (Photograph by Geoff Mayor.)

*Woman* of June 1892 (no connection with today's periodical of that name), edited by Arnold Bennett, kept readers abreast of the latest in bathing dresses.

The face that
launched the
horrors of the
1914–18 war
gazes
innocuously
from the cosy
cover of *Home
Chat*, 16 Nov.
1907.

problem . . . is one of the chief social difficulties of the present enlightened age. To make domestic service a profession . . . would bring a speedy termination to the pending famine which threatens the dissolution of comfortable home life, where servants are a necessity.'

For those fortunate enough to bring home alive one of this rare species, the routine—as established by *Homes and Gardens*—was as follows:

'She comes at 9 a.m. Steps first occupy her attention. She then washes up the supper and breakfast things. Second duty, to clean brass. This must be done every day. Flue-cleaning is one of her weekly tasks. She goes at 3 p.m. She is paid . . . 6d. an hour. She has her breakfast before she arrives. At 11 o'clock she stops work for ten minutes . . . for a cup of tea or cocoa with bread and butter, or margarine, and potted meat or jam. She has dinner at 1 o'clock. It is pretty certain she will not undertake to do any washing or ironing, and the housewife, of course, will certainly not contemplate doing it herself! This means outside help in the form of a washerwoman. Her charge is 4s. a day for eight hours.'

Another 'still available help' was the charwoman at 3s. 6d. a day—'and a conscientious char can do an astonishing amount of heavy work in a day'. But with chars becoming more and more disenchanted with 'the astonishingly heavy work' required of them for trifling rewards, women turned increasingly to mechanical aids.

It was the beginning of the long love-affair between the housewife and her household gadgets. Before then, a broom was a broom, a wash-tub a wash-tub, carpet-beaters, mops, dusters, scrubbing brushes distasteful objects consigned below-stairs. To have claimed acquaintance with any of them was tantamount to social suicide. Conversely the new appliances conferred a social status symbol previously equated with the number of one's servants.

Electricity took pride of place in the game of one-upmanship. 'Electricity in the home—what magic hovers about those words!' *Homes and Gardens* proclaims ecstatically, and enlarges upon the wonders of the new electric light, electric grills, kettles, heaters, fires, irons. 'Unfortunately the new electric vacuum cleaner' was not as yet, 'practical politics' in the home.

Objects now prized were then rejected or disguised.

'Brass bedsteads are not very desirable, but they can be converted . . . by having a wooden casting made to drop over the head and foot, and covered with a fabric such as chintz.'

That 'candlestick telephones' are now specially manufactured 'objects d'art' would have astonished those early *Homes and Gardens* readers. They were told:

'The telephone is a distinctly unbeautiful instrument, and your desire to conceal it is not uncommon.' The instrument could be 'effectively accommodated in a recess in a wall covered with a panel'—or hidden under 'a crinoline lady'. The now trendy Venetian blinds were another twenties throw-out. In a novel of that name by Ethel Mannin, they epitomised all that was narrow and repressive in the preceding era.

# CHAPTER NINE

# *The Twenties to the Seventies*

THE grim post-Great War years, the thirties Depression, the deprivations of the 1939–45 Second World War, were followed by an unprecedented demand for consumer products, a 'never had it so good' prosperity which in turn reacted upon the women's magazine market.

Mass production, widening educational and career prospects for women, full employment and the Welfare State transformed life for the average person beyond the most optimistic dreams of the early reformers. Home ownership, bathrooms, telephones, cars, television, holidays abroad, refrigerators, vacuum cleaners, washing machines, good clothing and a plentiful supply of (pre-Common Market) reasonably priced food, were no longer the prerogative of the comparatively wealthy, but within the accepted expectations of the majority. Of even greater significance perhaps was the new biological and economic freedom obtained by women, thanks to the introduction of the cheap, easily available contraceptive.

Adjusting to social change, catering for the new, prosperous teenage market, without estranging an older readership, coping with economic booms, recessions, stop-go policies, mergers, internal politics, 'experts', the pressures of big business and backroom accountants, demanded editorial contortions which for many magazines proved fatal.

Among the twenties' non-survivors *Eve* was a monthly 'devoted to a record of the Upper Classes'. Snippets include: 'Aeroplane holidays are becoming quite fashionable. More men are wearing corsets. Mr Henry Ford is producing 6,000 cars daily.' It also carried the first women's motoring feature, and (2 May 1923) ads for the then popular Atlantic liners.

*Modern Woman* (1925), more recently 'folded', described 'items indispensable to a comfortable bedroom' as 'an easy chair, well-lit dressing table, long mirror, gas fire, eiderdown, fur-edged boots and a ridiculously decorative boudoir cap'. 'If our bedrooms were as attractive as those of our Parisian sisters', it claimed, 'we would be less inclined to suffer from nerves.'

'Nerves', along with other ailments, received attention in most women's magazines from anonymous male practitioners. Only *Woman's Friend* (1924–50) struck a feminist note with their 'Dr Mary'.

Some twenties journals still flourishing are *Woman and Home* (1926) and *Woman's Journal* (1927). *Woman's Own*—now a giant weekly, amalgamating *Home Notes* and

THE
# WOMAN'S WEEKLY

THE PAPER *for* EVERY WOMAN

**1D**

THE PAPER *for* EVERY HOME

No. 1.—Vol. 1.          ONE PENNY.    EVERY WEDNESDAY.          November 4th, 1911.

*Woman's Weekly*, still topping the sales charts, first appeared 4 Nov. 1911.

```
1919
Aug 9   3 sheets              1  6
        3 bolster slips          9
        4 pillow cases        1  0
        1 pants                  4
        1 vest (gent's)          4
        1 pyjamas                8
        2 prs socks             4
        7 hanks (gent's)         7
        5 soft shirts         1  6
        2 ... collars            3
        4 linen                  8
        3 nightdresses        1  3
        3 combinations        1  3
        3 chemises            1  0
        3 drawers             1  4½
        6 prs stockings       1  0
        6 petticoats          3  0
        6 blouses             4  0
        4 aprons (linen)        10
        4  "   (morning)         8
        1 cotton dress           6
        2 overalls            1  4
        3 serviettes             4½
        2 tray cloths            6
        2 afternoon do.          7
       18 hanks (ladies)      1  6
        4 bath towels         1  4
        4 toilet do.          1  0
        1 round do.              4
        1 tablecloth (dining rm) 6
        1   "    (kitchen)       4
                            £ 1 10 7
```

Laundry bill, 1919. The alternative was to 'do it yourself'. (Photographs by courtesy of *Homes and Gardens*.)

*Woman's Day* — was first published in 1932. *Mother* (monthly), launched two years later, enjoys continued popularity.

Cosmetics were suspect well into the thirties. A letter in the now defunct monthly, *Housewife* (September 1934) comments: 'There is real truth in the complaint made by many wives that they must not annoy their husbands by wearing "make-up", although smart women who do so are admired by their husbands for their chic.'

Except in the industrial north where women mill-hands were traditional, employment was barred to married women by most industries. Wholly dependent on their husbands, they had as a *Good Housekeeping* of the day reveals, either to cajole or bully them into providing even a mere £1 deposit for that new home-help—the vacuum cleaner.

'I've had just about enough of working a twelve-hour day while you work eight!' declares a mutinous wife. 'Your office equipment is 1934 while I'm still working in 1834.'

Whatever the shortcomings of her household equipment, *Good Housekeeping* readers could not fault their fiction. Under the editorship of Miss Alice Head, contributors included Stella Gibbons, Raphael Sabatini, Winifred Holtby, St John Irvine, Eric Linklater, Francis Brett Young, James Hilton and Frank Swinnerton.

'Delicacy' and 'sensibility' had long been succeeded by 'Oomph' and 'It'—the

144

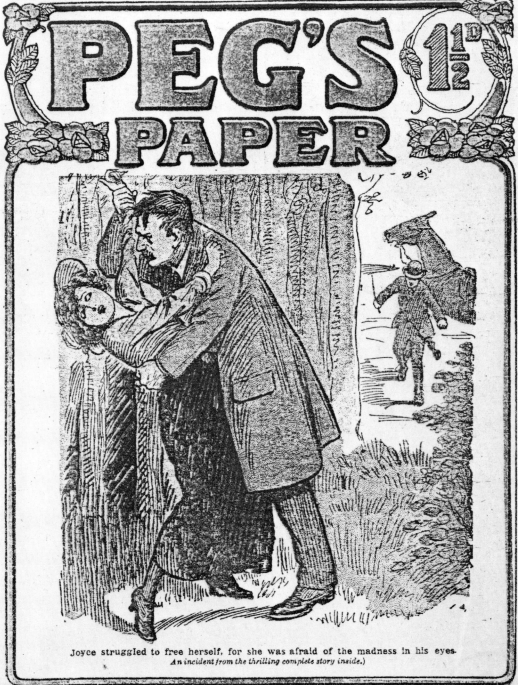

**"WHEN A WICKED MAN LOVES."**

# PEG'S PAPER

1½D

Joyce struggled to free herself, for she was afraid of the madness in his eyes.
*An incident from the thrilling complete story inside.)*

No. 2.

## LONG COMPLETE NOVEL INSIDE.

Nell Kennedy, originator of *Peg's Paper*, was adept at capturing and captioning the 'psychological moment' of her engrossing fiction.

145

Slick, svelte and the height of the twenties fashion – plus the 'short hair most men professed to detest'. (From a Harpers' Bazaar, English edition, fashion illustration. (Photograph by Jane Bridgeman.)

latter being the invention of twenties novelist Elinor Glynn, author of the 'daring'
*Three Weeks*. But if girls no longer dreamed of 'becoming ladies' they could still be
flattered by the snob-appeal of upper-crust patronage. A typical beauty ad of the
period reads:

'Here you see Lady Helena ——. Her eyes are blue and sparkling; a gleam of
auburn lights her golden hair, and her beauty is enhanced by a perfect skin, rose-
pink, and creamy-white and very fair indeed. "I have a beauty secret", she says, "and
it is a secret every girl can share. I use ——'s Cold Cream." '

*Woman*, today's giant weekly, first published 1 June 1937, price 2d., led the field in
colour-printing. Its initial issue carried hard-hitting articles from Labour M.P. Ellen
Wilkinson, and Margaret Lane. Pearl Buck, Noel Coward, and A. J. Cronin were
among its fiction writers. Beverley Nichols, a regular contributor, joined the ranks
of grandmother worshippers. 'Grandmother really knew how to play. She was a
mass of engaging accomplishments. She could paint water-colours, she could speak
French and German. Despite being burdened with quantities of petticoats, tight
corset and whalebone collars, she could cope with enormous kitchen ranges.'

At a time when, as *Good Housekeeping* recalls, 'Just before the war (1939) the
malnutrition figure of the population of Great Britain reached the appalling figure of

'Just now our young and pretty girls are pushing the craze for shorter skirts to the utmost limit' observed a scandalised *Daily Mail*. But short skirts were consistent with war-time economy.

148

The Prince of Wales (later Duke of Windsor) was every girl's 'dream lover'. *Good Housekeeping*, December 1922, by courtesy of The National Magazine Company. (Photograph by Jane Bridgeman.)

*The*
*Royal Bachelor*
*at Home*

By Walter T. Roberts

one-third' women were more concerned with trying to make ends meet, than with 'accomplishments'. Unlike contemporary women's magazine fiction, best-sellers such as *Woman of Glenshiels* by Lennox Kerr, *Angel Pavement* by J. B. Priestley and *Love on the Dole* by Walter Greenwood, reflected the conditions of the day.

Nor was it the Spanish Civil War (1936), the rising menace of Nazi Germany, or the Russian invasion of Finland (1939), that perturbed the *Woman's Pictorial*, but the 'servant problem which was discussed round nearly every afternoon tea-table.' This monthly, possibly because periodicals are planned far ahead, did not catch up with the war until November 1939, when Godfrey Winn—a first-rate journalist,

Snob appeal made more impact than sex-appeal in the still class-ridden thirties.

*Jeune Fille*
*turns into lovely lady in three days*

AT SIXTEEN she was a slim fair girl who escaped from house and town whenever she could — to ride her pony up hill and down dale.

"But one day a white satin gown arrived for my first hunt ball," says Lady Oranmore. "I tried it on — and heavens! my face didn't match my arms and shoulders at all. Such weather-beaten skin! And the ball so near!

"It was my governess told me about Pond's Creams. I used them, and in three days my skin became as soft and smooth as if I'd given it a season of care. Ever since, I've used Pond's Creams," Lady Oranmore adds. . . . And you've only to look at her to see how lovely they have kept her complexion!

*You* can have a skin as lovely as Lady Oranmore's. Pond's Creams are easy to use and this is how they will work to make your skin so beautiful:

### Rough skin turned satin-soft at once

Wind and sun are constantly drying your skin. Raw little edges break free! And whether your skin is dry, oily, or normal, it soon looks dull and coarse.

Now Pond's Vanishing Cream contains the substance found in beautiful young skin which makes it soft and smooth. When you use Pond's Vanishing Cream, this substance is absorbed by your skin, making it like velvet.

Also, there is a second substance in Pond's Vanishing Cream. This *nourishes*, makes your skin firm, corrects drooping contours, fills out lines. Spread on Pond's Vanishing Cream *always* before you powder. It will make your powder go on smoothly and hold it for hours, while it keeps your skin soft and fresh. Use this cream at night, to beautify your skin as you sleep.

But, first, always cleanse with Pond's *Cold* Cream. Use it every night. It clears out the pores and stimulates your *under-skin* so that blackheads, blemishes and enlarged pores disappear. Start using Pond's Creams today. **Pond's**

**MILDRED, LADY ORANMORE AND BROWNE**

150

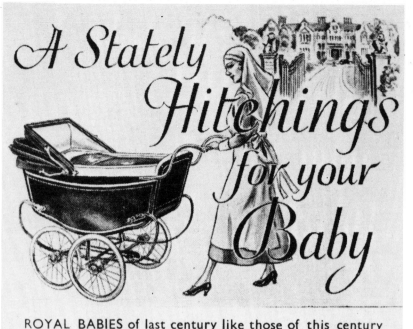

# A Stately Hitchings for your Baby

ROYAL BABIES of last century like those of this century
rode in Hitchings Baby Coaches.
BRITISH and Foreign Royalty, Nobility and Gentry know
what is right, so they choose a Hitchings.
   RR on a Motor Car stands for perfection so HITCHINGS
on a Baby Coach means—no equal, anywhere, at any price.
Quiet Dignity, Style, Elegance, Comfort and Dependability
are outstanding features of
   THE STATELY HITCHINGS.
As in days gone by, the superlative
Hitchings stands unchallenged as the
   PREMIER BABY COACH.

   Write for Catalogue B3.

*A Hitchings of Bygone Days*

## HITCHINGS & COMPANY,
495, OXFORD ST., LONDON, W.I.
(Near Marble Arch)

Kon-tayn-al Ltd.

The patronage
of 'royalty,
nobility and
gentry' was
somewhat
astonishingly
thought to
appeal to the
mothers of the
Depressed
1930s.
By courtesy of
Jack
Hampshire,
Baby Carriage
Collection,
Biddenden,
Kent.

proclaimed adroitly, 'We are two months nearer peace.' Concern for pets was
paramount. 'Give your pets a dose of sedative before an air raid' readers were told,
'and send for the official pamphlet containing suggestions for war-time diet for cats
and dogs'.

   More realistically, Mary Grieve, editing *Woman*, interpreted for readers the
plethora of regulations, restrictions, instructions, relating to everything from child
evacuees to black-outs, air raid procedures, fire-watching, voluntary services,
rationing, billeting, clothing coupons, travel restrictions, Service grants, with
which readers were suddenly confronted. By contrast, magazine fiction remained
curiously impervious to the contemporary scene. If the problems of girls called up

When the waves ruled Britain. A thirties ad from *Woman's Magazine*. (Photograph by Geoff Mayor.)

## YOU *CAN* SET YOUR WAVES AT HOME

The BUTYWAVE WAVESETTER, designed by one of the most skilful of our modern hairdressers, will set your waves, exactly and naturally. Its action is entirely automatic—there are no "messy" processes—no steam—no gas—no metal parts—nothing to make the hair brittle or weak—nothing to "pull" and give headaches.

## ADJUSTED IN A SECOND TO YOUR OWN STYLE

No matter what style of hairdressing you adopt, the BUTYWAVE WAVESETTER can be adjusted to accord with it in a few seconds. If you glance at the pictures a moment you will see how simple it is. The pictures are actual photographs taken during a test. You can see how quickly her hair was pressed gently into deep natural waves. These waves lasted more than two days and that after only wearing the BUTYWAVE WAVESETTER for 45 minutes.

## SO COMFORTABLE YOU CAN SLEEP IN IT

The BUTYWAVE WAVESETTER has no metal parts. Nothing to dig in the head. You will hardly know you've got it on, it's so comfortable. You can sleep with it on your head in complete comfort.

## YOU SAVE MONEY TOO

Think! 5/-, the cost of the BUTYWAVE WAVESETTER, is all you have to pay for years of home Wavesetting and no inconvenience of periodical visits to the hairdresser.

**BUTYWAVE**
WAVESETTER
BRITISH MADE
**5/-**
OBTAINABLE FROM ALL HIGH-CLASS DRAPERS, CHEMISTS AND HAIRDRESSERS, AND ALL BRANCHES OF BOOTS'
In case of difficulty, post coupon to the Butywave Co., 10 Tachbrook Street, London, S.W.1
Manufactured under licence by the Butywave Company. English Patent Number 328215. Foreign Patents applied for.

## SET YOUR

It doesn't matter if your hair is straight (like this girl's)—it doesn't matter how obstinate it is, the BUTYWAVE WAVESETTER will make a wonderful difference to it in a very short time. You'll be surprised at the lovely deep natural-looking waves it gives. There's no fuss or bother, no gas, steam, electricity or hot irons. It's just as simple as A B C.

## OWN HAIR

First of all damp your hair with Water or Setting Lotion. Then slip the cap on your head, bonnet fashion, making sure that the central cross-piece follows the line of your parting. You adjust the cross-pieces by pulling them along the elastic supports. Now hold the cap by the ribbons and pull down, bringing the hands just below the ears (see picture No. 2), then . . . .

## AT HOME!

release the ribbons slowly. Fasten the cap loosely under the chin. Now see what happens! (Picture No. 3.) As you let the ribbons go the cross-pieces have automatically gathered up the hair and pressed it gently into waves. Just pinch the waves with the fingers and leave the cap on until the hair is quite dry, remove front first and . . . .

## LIKE THIS...

here's the result! (Picture No. 4.) A head of lovely wavy hair. See how natural-looking the waves are. Everyone will think you've had it permed—and so you have. These beautiful waves won't comb or brush out, and when you wash your hair you only have to slip the cap on again for a short time to bring the waves back to their full glory.

Wholesale Agents for Chemists and Hairdressers :
THE BUTYWAVE CO., 10 Tachbrook Street, S.W.1

Wholesale Agents for Drapery Trade :
CHAPPELL, ALLEN & CO., LTD., 136-7 London Wall, E.C.2

To the Butywave Co., 10 Tachbrook Street, London, S.W.1.

Dear Sir,—Please send me by return one of your BUTYWAVE HOME WAVING CAPS, for which I enclose postal order for 5/-.

Name .....................................

Address .................................

# Good Housekeeping

**JANUARY 1937 · ONE SHILLING**

## CARDINAL SECRETS OF SUCCESS *by* CANON *"DICK"* SHEPPARD

*A. J. Cronin · James Hilton · Margaret Lane*
*Frank Swinnerton · S. P. B. Mais*

Top authors contributed to *Good Housekeeping*'s success under the (then) editorship of Alice Head.

No 1 issue of Woman's Realm, in which Fiction Editor Mary Irvine initiated a new era of realistic stories. By courtesy of IPC Magazines.

WOMAN'S REALM

4D EVERY TUESDAY
Week ending
February 22, 196[]

No.1

EXTRA

8 page pull-out booklet of NEW knitting patterns

Four Lovely Lipsticks for You! see page 24

154

for the Services, manning anti-aircraft guns, driving ambulances, serving as Air Raid wardens or Firemen, or of women left alone to cope with families, were mentioned, it was usually to sustain the belief that despite the presence of troops from all over the world, wives and sweethearts remained faithful; that absent husbands and lovers were equally true; that girls and young men faced with parting and the possibility of death never, however tempted, slept together unless married.

*Woman's Pictorial*, having told readers that 'the W A A F (Women's Auxiliary Air Force) learner-drivers were as keen as mustard', returned to the more urgent topic of 'how to embroider a baby's napkin ring'. Not one that appealed to a reader who confessed, 'the very idea of having a baby in this dreadful war is ruining the thought of my approaching marriage.' Not for her, reassuring advice on contraceptives, family planning. She is rebuked: 'You must trust life more. If you have so little faith in the future for which millions are fighting, what right have you to the peace when it comes?'

Stalingrad, one of the grimmest battles of the Second World War, is reduced to a cosy-corner pet story in the issue of 20 Feb. 1943: 'I wonder if you heard of Murka the cat who helped the Red Army fire, for Stalingrad? For three days clever Murka was a "messenger girl" for two Red Army soldiers. The soldiers were isolated at the top of a tall building overlooking the enemy lines. Murka, sent for a meal to the base kitchen three streets away, delivered messages directing the artillery where to fire.'

Wartime experience widened women's outlook and expectations. Cosmetics, no longer the 'badge' of the prostitute, or even 'annoying husbands', became big business. Sex, enthroned, was exploited to sell everything from a ball of wool to a back-boiler. The dichotemy between magazine feature articles and fiction, magazine fiction and television drama became increasingly apparent. It was not until 1958 with the publication of *Woman's Realm* that Mary Irvine, under the editorship of Joyce Ward, initiated the break-through from the traditional saccharine to more realistic type fiction.

A further blast of fresh air came with the transfer of Marjorie Proops 'witty, pithy and wise' advice column from the *Daily Mirror* to *Woman's Mirror*, published in 1962.

Underestimating the strength of traditional values and old loyalties led publishing houses to summon the services of one Dr Ernest Dichter Ph.D. a Viennese psychologist known as 'Freud with an order book . . . whose policies in advising American advertisers to interpret readers' subconscious desires earned him a fortune . . . and many critics'. The resultant over-emphasis on sex and sensationalism led to the downfall of *Woman's Mirror*—and of the initially brilliant monthly, *Nova* (launched 1965).

More perceptively, Patricia Lamburn (daughter of *Peg's Paper* originator Nell Kennedy and journalist F. J. Lamburn), aware that 'vast numbers of women, confused by changing values, sought guidance and reassurance', launched her Confession weeklies: *Hers, True Romance,* and *True.* Simply written and based on realistic situations with which readers could identify, they proved an instant success.

'Witty, pithy and wise' Marjorie Proops established the most popular ever, new-style advice column, first in the *Daily Herald* and subsequently in *Woman's Mirror* and *Daily Mirror*. (Photograph by Geoff Mayor.)

# Dear Marje

**Dear Marje**

WHAT would you do with a family of men who start a conversation and, if I join in, say: "I wasn't talking to you?" I know they don't mean it unkindly, but it gets my goat.

LOVING MUM

### Dear Mum

It's got my goat, too, in sympathy. Remind these thoughtless menfolk that this is the twentieth century and way beyond the belief that the little woman should be seen and not heard. You're an individual with ideas of your own, and just you go right ahead and prove it.

**Dear Marje**

IN order to attract members of the opposite sex, do you have to be plain and intellectual or beautiful and brainless? I often wonder.

BLONDE

### Dear Blonde

Just be yourself . . . That way you will attract the kind of man who prefers you to any other type.

**Dear Marje**

WHAT can I do to get my husband to go on a diet? He is no longer the slim, handsome man I fell in love with, but when I tell him about being tubby, he gets angry and says he likes being that way.

SLENDER

### Dear Slender

Psychiatrists would say that some people who over-eat are hungry, not for food, but for love and affection. Maybe if, instead of criticising his waistline, you put your arm round it occasionally, he would want to regain his slim and handsome appearance.

**Dear Marje**

I GET so depressed—and discouraged from buying—when I go into a shoe shop and see the sloppy, untidy, shabby, footwear worn by the salesgirls. Don't you think it would be a good idea if they were given free shoes by their firms to wear when on duty?

DAINTY

### Dear Dainty

How would you like to be on your feet all day, running in and out of the stockrooms, hopping up and down ladders and trying to please customers who can't make up their ruddy minds? You'd want to wear your most comfortable old shoes too. However, I'll agree that it would be a good idea if shoe firms supplied assistants with really comfortable but smart footwear.

**Dear Marje**

RECENTLY I saw a young couple in a restaurant feeding each other with ice-cream. Can you beat this for sloppiness?

OBSERVER

### Dear Observer

I'm right with you. That was taking spooning much too far.

**Dear Marje**

FOR the past six months I've had a constant partner at a jiving club. Now the club has closed down, and when my dancing boy friend sees me he almost ignores me. What can I do to show him that I care for him?

UNWANTED

### Dear Unwanted

I reckon it hardly matters what you do to show him you care. Since he appears not to care back, you're wasting valuable time which could be spent in joining another club and looking for another boy . . . one who wants to partner you on—and off—the dance floor.

**Dear Marje**

A FRIEND with two children maintains that an addition to her family would be a luxury. I say that her car, telephone and other things are luxuries and that if she really wanted a third child she could give these up. What's your opinion?

INTERESTED

### Dear Interested

My opinion is that the size of other people's families is none of my business—or yours.

**Dear Marje**

I AM sixteen and my mother allows me to go out with my boy friends, but she will not hear of my going into their homes to play records. She says it isn't right to go unchaperoned into a boy's house until you're at least engaged. I don't agree, do you?

POPPY

### Dear Poppy

Your mum knows you better than I do. Perhaps she has reasons for playing safe.

**Dear Marje**

MY wife is mad on knitting. She carries her plain and purl all over the house, and you can even tell which room she's in by following the noise of the needles. Now she's started knitting at the cinema and at friends' houses. What can I do?

CAST OFF

### Dear Cast

Buy her a deluxe knitting machine with all the latest gadgets. It's not exactly handbag size and it will ensure that everywhere your wife goes, her knitting certainly won't in future.

**Dear Marje**

MY hubby persists in wearing a shabby old sports coat he's had for 16 years. When I hinted that the time had come for them to part he replied that he'd had his coat much longer than he'd been married to me. What chance has a wife got against an old coat?

RIVA

### Dear Riva

A better chance than she has against a young bit of stuff.

**Dear Marje**

A LITTLE while ago I was going out regularly with a young man. But he kept on so much about wanting to settle down and get married, I decided to break off with him —because I wished to stay single.

Just recently I learned that he has a wife and was evidently trying to lead me on. How can a girl know when a man is married, when he so convincingly tells her he is single?

SQUASHED

### Dear Squashed

You should worry. If I were you I'd sit and gloat over my lucky escape—and make sure you check up on future wooers.

**Dear Marje**

SEEMS to me that when it comes to making a go of marriage, the onus is placed on us wives all the time. We're constantly told: "How to keep your man. How to make your marriage a success. . . . If he comes home dejected and dispirited cheer him and help him rebuild his morale."

I ask you, is a wife a slave? I notice nobody ever tells men how to treat and keep a wife happy. Do you agree women should always be the subservient towards their husbands?

DEFIANT

### Dear Defiant

You couldn't ask this question of a less subservient wife. No "yes" girl am I. I never stick to the rules as laid down by marriage guidance experts. And at the time of writing, my spouse seems fairly satisfied with the rough treatment he gets—touch wood.

**Dear Marje**

SOMEHOW I seem to attract all the Weary Willies and Neverwells, and I have to stand for hours listening to stories of their aches and pains. I'm not really unsympathetic, but I get so tired of "organ recital." Any advice, apart from wearing a disguise?

WEARY

### Dear Weary

Pull out all the stops and get cracking with some pointed repartee, like "And how's what's left of YOU this morning, Mrs. ——?" However, I'm always prepared to hear a genuine case as I think it makes the other party feel better and me darned grateful to be alive and well

21

156

At the opposite end of the spectrum, *Cosmopolitan* (monthly), an American (Hearst) publication, commands a healthy circulation under editor Deirdre McSharry. A magazine 'for young women who like to be treated as adults' its bosomy cover-girls and glossy-magazine presentation sugar-coat an amount of crisply written, sociological material.

*Spare Rib*, launched in 1972 and run on a shoe-string by a collective editorial of dedicated young women and unpaid contributors, is a brave, campaigning successor of *The Woman Worker* (1908) and the Suffragette *Dreadnought* (1915) in tackling problems elsewhere swept under editorial mats.

Among survivors who kept their heads and their readers throughout the traumatic decades, are *The Lady*, *Woman's Weekly*, *Good Housekeeping*, *Homes and Gardens*, *Harpers and the Queen*, and *Vogue*. Explaining *The Lady*'s continued popularity, editor Joan Graham says, 'We deliberately select the best that the seventies has to offer, while rejecting the worst.' That *Woman's Weekly* has celebrated its Diamond Jubilee and commands the highest circulation among the weeklies, editor Mary Dilnot attributes to the journal's being 'tailor-made to readers' tastes, the loved and familiar'. *Good Housekeeping*, first published in March 1922, 'in a Britain of gas-street lighting, steam radio, ankle-length dresses and coal fires' and edited today by Miss Charlotte Lessing, 'retains its appeal to the intelligent woman from the twenties to the sixties, covering every aspect of life.'

*Homes and Gardens* has a similarly informed, timeless readership. Modernised after 1945 by Lady Georgina Coleridge—who pioneered articles on antiques—it remains popular under today's editor Miss Psyche Pirie. *Vogue* and *Harpers and the Queen* retain their appeal, with superb presentation, for the fashionable avante garde.

While features and fiction have changed marginally throughout the centuries, the time-honoured 'Agony column' has altered beyond recognition. Contraception, women's financial independence, the break-up of family life, easier divorce and a changed moral climate brought an unprecedented pressure of responsibility upon women's magazine's advice columnists. Where earlier writers could pronounce judgment based on ex-cathedra certitudes, religious teachings, entrenched social shibboleths, their successors, Marjorie Proops, Evelyn Home (Peggy Makins), Clare Sheridan, Anna Raeburn, and Mary Grant, among others, are faced with problems previous generations dared not voice, and which no longer admit of cut and dried solutions.

Mary Grieve, editor of *Woman* from the late thirties to the sixties recalls 'cries from mothers bogged down by rules and regulations . . . by people in legal messes, by people in emotional despair, by women sick . . . of their hair, their figures, their wallpaper; by people whose pastry is heavy, whose knitting is all awry, whose holidays were a flop, whose confidence is gone'.

Marjorie Proops, a lady not noticeably given to 'the vapours' writes in her book *Dear Marje* (published by André Deutsch) 'If, way back in my *Herald* days, I'd had a letter from a woman asking how her man's technique can be improved to ensure her satisfactory orgasm, I'd have fainted dead away on the office floor.'

Some
women's
magazines of
the 1960s.

**EVERYWOMAN**

SEPTEMBER 1966, 2s.

TOTALLY New
TOTALLY Gay
Fashion gets the
TOTAL LOOK

ENCHANTED ISLES
of GALAPAGOS
and the strangest
animals on earth

YOUR DATE WITH
THE BEAUTY
MAKERS

SEX, ME and MY FAMILY by SHIRLEY MACLAINE

# PETTICOAT

19th AUGUST 1967 ONE SHILLING

## THE NEW YOUNG WOMAN

**BELMONDO:** the marvellous machine
**BODIES:** final beauty analysis
**BASICS:** fashion below the belt
## AND THE PLAIN FACTS ABOUT DIVORCE

160

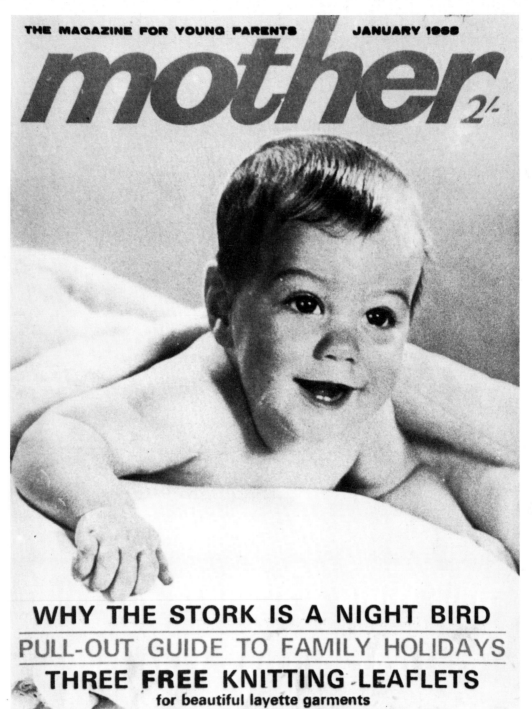

THE MAGAZINE FOR YOUNG PARENTS   JANUARY 1968

# mother

2/-

## WHY THE STORK IS A NIGHT BIRD
### PULL-OUT GUIDE TO FAMILY HOLIDAYS
### THREE FREE KNITTING LEAFLETS
for beautiful layette garments

Another IPC 'baby' still going strong. By courtesy of IPC.

Following in the tradition of the *Dreadnought*, *Spare Rib* campaigns for women's lib and for improving working and social conditions.

A WOMEN'S LIBERATION MAGAZINE MARCH 1977   ISSUE 56   30 PENCE

# spare Rib

**Simone de Beauvoir Interviewed**

"Its Colditz or the concrete jungle" Taking on Liverpool Council

162

Today, her postbags bring queries on abortion, alcoholism, lesbianism, homosexuality, incest, wife-battering, bestiality, cries of help from transvestites, from men anxious about the size of their penises, from women worried about their breasts, their vaginas, and, to quote Marjorie Proops, 'queries about orgasms are as commonplace as those about mothers-in-law'. She continues: 'In the twenty years or so since I started handing out advice in newspaper and magazine columns, I estimate that close to a million people have written to me. Add to that the immense number of those who have written to . . . other columnists . . . and you are bound to reach the sobering conclusion that we fill (or endeavour to fill) a vast need which neither the religious bodies, nor the social services, the doctors or psychiatrists, the welfare workers or the voluntary help organisations can, it seems, adequately answer.'

It is equally certain that millions more, non-corresponding readers have gained help and reassurance from such advice. And if, over the centuries, women's magazines have brought to generations of readers comfort, entertainment, enlightenment, and a harmless escapism, surely this is no mean achievement.

# Women behind-scenes

Lady Georgina Coleridge, former editor *Homes and Gardens*
Mary Dilnot, editor *Woman's Weekly*
Mary Grieve, former editor *Woman*
Alice Head, former editor *Nash's Magazine, Homes and Gardens*, etc.
Evelyn Home (Peggy Makins) former editor *Woman* problem page
Mary Irvine, former fiction editor *Woman's Realm*
Margaret Koumi, editor *19*
Patricia Lamburn, director IPC
Charlotte Lessing, editor *Good Housekeeping*
Deirdre McSharry, editor *Cosmopolitan*
Marjorie Proops, advice columnist (formerly *Woman's Mirror*) *Daily Mirror*
Jane Reed, editor *Woman's Own*
Josephine Sandilands, editor *Woman*
Lesley Saxby, former fiction editor, *Woman's Mirror*, consultant fiction editor
     *Woman's Own*
Monica Tyson, editor *Woman's Realm*

What makes a women's magazine 'tick'? Why does one magazine flourish, while another, presumably based on a similar formula, 'folds'? It is axiomatic in women's magazine circles that 'it is the editor who makes the magazine'. Likewise that there could be as many different types of women's magazines as there are different types of women. The following brief interviews with some successful women's journals' editors may help to provide some of the answers.

*Lady Georgina Coleridge*
Accepting the premise that, as Lady Georgina Coleridge phrased it, 'it is the person who makes the magazine' it is not difficult to understand the success of the periodicals she has edited or directed.
*Homes and Gardens*, and *Woman's Journal* have each reflected her infectiously warm, out-going personality; combined her flair for anticipating the needs and moods of the middle-income-group woman reader, achieved a higher than usual literary content, and an above-average, yet attainable standard of home furnishings, decor,

fashion, beauty and cookery, while avoiding the out-of-this-world snobbishness that too often afflicts 'the glossies'.

'A high quality that remains stable, yet keeps in tune with the times, aimed at a generation with a long-time spectrum' proved the successful inspiration of a career that began almost accidentally. 'Soon after leaving school, I met a woman working on *Harper's Bazaar* at a luncheon party. She asked what I intended doing. Stuck for a reply, I said—journalism. She told me to try writing for *Harper's Bazaar*. I'd never heard of it!'

Three articles written that same afternoon on her father's club's writing paper, were accepted. So too were further features. While she was still under-age, *Harper's* recognised her organising ability and enthusiasm sufficiently to entrust her with her own office and staff to sell magazine subscriptions, and later, advertising. Her association with the magazine finished in 1939, to be followed by war service at the Foreign Office.

'Then on D Day I walked round to the office of *Country Life*, and asked my old boss, Miss Alice Head, editor of *Homes and Gardens*, for a job. She said, "Come back when the war is really over"—and I did just that.' From 1945–49 Lady Georgina was assistant fashion and beauty editor of *Homes and Gardens*, anonymous beauty editor of *Country Life*. On Miss Alice Head's retirement in 1949, she took over the editorship (until 1963) of *Homes and Gardens*. 'Miss Head had made a marvellous job of re-vamping what had been a purely architectural magazine, into a women's journal, but had been handicapped by the paper shortage, and lack of colour pages. I was lucky enough to have more scope, so was able to revitalise and bring the magazine into the sixties.'

Again, following in Miss Head's footsteps, she was appointed the only female director of Country Life Ltd. in 1963, and of George Newnes shortly afterwards. From 1966–69 she was both editor and publisher of *Homes and Gardens* and publisher of *Woman's Journal*, and of *Ideal Home* 'for two years or so', and from 1971–74 director of Special Projects for IPC.

Long before it became a popular subject she had introduced articles and an advice column in *Homes and Gardens* on antiques, and broke new ground in the same journal with the introduction of a wine club. In passing, it may also be mentioned that *Homes and Gardens* is almost unique in having successfully abandoned the glamour-girl close-up cover now almost traditional among women's magazines.

In 1968, Lady Georgina was likewise responsible as editor/publisher for giving 'a more positive image' to *Woman's Journal*. She pays enthusiastic tribute to her successors; on *Homes and Gardens*, Mrs Psyche Pirie (former furnishing editor of the magazine); Miss Kathleen Jones editing *Woman's Journal*, and Mr Willie Landels, editor of *Harper's and Queen*—'where it all began. They are all doing splendid work.'


*Mary Dilnot, Editor of Woman's Weekly*
Miss Mary Dilnot, who comes of a journalistic family, arrived at *Woman's Weekly*

'in the lovely, happy days when you did everything from making the tea to lay-out and subbing'.

It was the year that the Second World War started, but after a short period with the ATS she returned to the magazine, working under 'that fantastic editor, Miss Biddy Johnson, who taught me everything I know'.

Shortly after, she was appointed deputy editor, but when the magazine was taken over in 1960 by the Daily Mirror Group, she found herself working under five different editors in two-and-a-half years.

In 1971, Miss Dilnot was appointed editor of *Woman's Weekly*, and recently was appointed to the Board of Directors of IPC Women's Magazines Group.

She attributes the magazine's success to its neighbourliness, its 'fondness for the familiar. If things don't change too much it can be very comforting.' That her own warmth and essential friendliness 'spills over' into the magazine, is obvious.

Its policy, as laid down in its first issue of 4 November 1911, still holds good. As Miss Biddy Johnson expressed it: 'First of all I should like to tell you that the dominant note throughout is usefulness. Our one desire is to please the average woman.'

Described as 'the little miracle of Fleet Street', *Woman's Weekly* not only recently celebrated its Diamond Jubilee, but its sales approached one and three quarter million, to achieve Britain's largest current, individual circulation among women's magazines.

Editorial office duties apart, Mary Dilnot likes to get out and meet her readers, even when it takes her as far from home as Australia and Canada, and until recently, on annual readers' cruises to Norway. 'Every one of our readers is such a nice person' she says, a compliment which readers meeting her would reciprocate.

*Mary Grieve*

Inevitably Miss Mary Grieve's story is the story of *Woman*, for it was she who edited and directed it through twenty-two years of its most difficult, and also its palmiest days.

Her appointment in 1937 to the associate editorship of *Woman*, (under editor John Gammie) at the age of thirty-one, followed journalistic experience in Glasgow, and on *Mother*.

First published in June of that year, *Woman* leapt from a million circulation in 1939 to over three million by 1962.

Mary Grieve recalls that in those early days 'there could be no casual reference to daily baths, telephones, holidays abroad, cars, refrigerators, vacuum cleaners. These things were not available to our readers.' Calories, vitamins, psychology, were terms unknown. Nor would the vast spectrum of sex and medical matters, now familiar to readers, have been acceptable.

*Woman*'s fiction permitted little beyond romances with happy endings, invariably equated with marriage. Divorce, any hint of unconventionality, was unmentionable, a prohibition imposed to avoid offending the Irish market, and 'disproportionate'

166

Mary Grieve felt, 'to the numbers affected. The Evelyn Home page particularly, had to be changed for the Irish readers.'

War-time saw *Woman*'s circulation shrink to three-quarters of a million, and twenty pages which were yet able to offer valuable service. As a government statement records:

'Without Government co-operation, the women's magazines are using their influence wisely and patriotically. It seems obvious they could perform a much greater national service if they had easily accessible facts.'

During the war years it was *Woman* which familiarised readers with Utility Furniture, the only new furniture then available.

Later, in 1948, the magazine acquainted readers with the intricacies of the July 1948 National Insurance Act, the National Health Act, the National Assistance Act and the Children's Act.

Apart from helping to improve the life-style and quality of women's lives, Mary Grieve holds that over the years, *Woman* has fulfilled the role of providing them with a friend.

*Alice Head*

No exception to the sad but incontrovertible fact that pioneers tend to go unhonoured and unsung, Miss Alice Head has probably done more to shape and influence the women's magazine scene than any woman editor before or since her time.

Born in 1886, her entry into journalism was not without home-background doubts.

'My mother wanted me to be a teacher, or to enter the Civil Service. I thought both terribly dull!'

Her father 'did not mind what she did, so long as it was honest'.

The climate of the times is best illustrated by the fact that when, in reply to a small ad she found herself secretary to *Country Life* editor, P. Anderson-Graham, he took her father out to lunch 'to assure him she was in good hands'.

After two years as secretary (in the same firm) to Lord Alfred Douglas of the Oscar Wilde court case 'fame', she was appointed, aged twenty-three, as 'England's youngest-ever editor' to the helm of the newly launched *Woman and Home*.

Three years later found her as acting editor of the British edition of *Nash's Magazine*, owned by the fabled American newspaper tycoon Mr Randolph Hearst 'a generous employer and a very kind and considerate man'.

The post not only carried an impressive salary—'My father said—"they must be mad!" — but likewise brought transatlantic travel, a chauffeur-driven limousine, and the responsibility of buying, staffing and entertaining at Randolph Hearst's castle at St Donat's, Wales. It also gave her the opportunity of commissioning such literary giants as George Bernard Shaw, H. G. Wells, Somerset Maugham, G. K. Chesterton, Compton Mackenzie, Marie Corelli and W. J. Locke among others.

She finds the greatest contrast between women's magazines then and now in 'the greatly improved, far more elaborate artistic production; the superior photography, lay-out and type-setting. Editorial content has changed little, except that today's magazines deal more openly with sex.'

It is a change of which she approves. 'Parents were very strict in my day. Children were kept very much in the dark.' She admits to having been 'in the dark' herself until aged thirty-four she reviewed a book by that pioneer of birth-control (and her old school-fellow), Dr Marie Stopes.

Another former school-fellow, Phillipa Fawcett, founded the non-violent wing of Women's Suffrage, which Alice Head joined.

'I had no intention of chaining myself to railings, that sort of thing!'

In 1920 she became the first-ever woman managing director of the National Magazine Company. From 1920–41 she founded and edited the British edition of *Good Housekeeping*. She was appointed a member of the Board of *Country Life* in 1941, and edited *Homes and Gardens* from 1941–49.

On retiring in 1949 she became treasurer and financial adviser of the City Temple, an honorary post which enabled her to prove her exceptional business acumen.

Now, in her nineties, and still taking an interest in women's magazines, she lives quietly in Chelsea.

### *Evelyn Home* (Peggy Makins)

Few women attain the distinction of having their name become a household word. Fewer still can hope to maintain the honour over decades. Yet this has been the achievement of 'Evelyn Home', who, for thirty-eight years provided readers of *Woman* with a shoulder to weep upon, a friend in need, an ever-ready adviser.

Ironically, Evelyn Home was a name invented in the office. 'Evelyn because of its associations with Eve. Home, for its similar, basic, feminine appeal.'

Peggy Makins, the writer behind the name and fame, is smallish, fairish, self-effacing. Unlike many of her contemporaries whose association with publishing was accidental, breaking into journalism was for Peggy a hard, six-year-long struggle.

'I began as a shorthand typist at the age of sixteen, did some freelance journalism, and encouraged by my mother kept writing to editors for jobs.'

Her perseverance was rewarded on 5 June 1937 when she was engaged on the editorial staff of *Woman*.

Like Juliet, who was not Romeo's first love, Peggy was not the first Evelyn Home, her predecessor being an exiled German psychologist. Her ambition was to become a dramatic critic, so when the original Evelyn Home left and Peggy was asked to replace her at a moment's notice, her reaction was one of dread. 'It was the last thing I wanted to do!'

Sharing her doubts was Mary Grieve, *Woman*'s editor. 'She thought I was too young and inexperienced for the job.' Terrified, but never one to duck a challenge, Peggy read up psychology in the public library, equipped herself to cope with the then weekly twenty to thirty letters. This intake swelled to thousands a year, and was explained by the intuitive warmth and sympathy she was able to give to readers whose acceptance of traditional standards she reinforced.

If in those early days she appeared to lean heavily on the side of conventionality, it was because she regards convention 'not as a corset, but as a support' within whose aegis society in general, and women in particular, achieve comparative security. Across the years she has struck a sensitive balance between sterner, outmoded mores, and a kindlier, more tolerant code, without falling backwards into the pitfalls of a confused permissiveness.

Oppressed at times by the sheer weight of other women's problems, especially 'by the amount of physical cruelty revealed in the letters', she has been compensated by the knowledge that she has been able to offer them helpful guide-lines.

After retiring from *Woman* in 1974, Peggy spent two years counselling by radio for the BBC.

*Mary Irvine*

That the general standard of fiction in today's women's magazines is higher than ever before, is due almost entirely to former fiction editor (and later consultant fiction editor) of *Woman's Realm*, Mrs Mary Irvine.

Mary Irvine, who now runs her own literary agency, entered journalism via the distinguished agents, Curtis Brown.

Soon after, invited to join the editorial staff of a popular publishing house, she found herself increasingly at odds with the prevailing, unquestioning assumption that all 'they', the readers, wanted fiction-wise was 'rose-tinted escapism'.

'Time and time again I had to reject first-class material because I was told "It isn't a story for our magazine." The tone of the office was ultra-lady-like. Most of the staff were university graduates with backgrounds far removed from that of our average readers. Stories centred round pretty, middle-class heroines married, or interested in middle-class, professional men. Any suggestion that a story might be set, say, in a depressed area, with a miner-hero, brought the response, "Our readers aren't interested in that sort of thing." '

By 1959, 'frustrated by eleven years of wallowing in sugary marshmallow', she was about to leave 'and get a job in Marks and Spencers' when she was persuaded to compete, successfully as it transpired, via a strenuous, three-months editorial stint for the post of fiction editor of the about-to-be-launched *Woman's Realm*.

It proved the turning point in her career, and a milestone in the history of women's magazine fiction.

'For the first time ever, we had stories with an East End or provincial background, women with whom our readers could identify. The response was tremendous.'

To the relief both of readers and writers, heroines no longer had to be young and beautiful. They could be plain, ugly, middle-aged, elderly, and again for the first time ever, halt, lame, blind or deaf. The one criterion was a good, readable story 'up to the standard of the Strand Magazine'.

Mary Irvine admits that initially she may have over-reacted.

'We went through all the illnesses, including cancer, which I would not do, today. Finally we went over the edge with a story about a mongol child, which roused questions in the House.' Summoned by the managing editor, she accepted with good grace, his stricture—'We are here to entertain, not to upset people.'

'From then on it was a case of striking a balance between realism and escapism, while still providing a market for the story with a downbeat ending.'

Mary pays whole-hearted tribute to her former editor Joyce Ward. 'She let everyone have a free hand. She was a wonderful editor whose name should be recorded in history.'

Since those days becoming a mother has given Mary a new slant on readership. 'Sitting behind an editorial desk gives you a sense of grandeur. You tend to become "godlike", to feel you *know*. It is not until you are at home all day with an infant that you appreciate the average woman's problems and outlook.'

### *Margaret Koumi, Editor of* 19

Attitudes rather than age-groups are what matter to Margaret Koumi, editor of the successful magazine *19*, started in 1968.

Readership covers girls 'between 17 and 26' with features aimed at whatever is of particular interest to any year, 'such as ecology, social changes, contraception, abortion etc. We keep ahead of fashion, but up to the minute with features. We try to educate and inform, and hopefully with all this we also entertain.'

Margaret's career began as secretary to the editor of a pop magazine called *Boyfriend*. From there she moved on to become a sub, then later she was a sub on *TV World* (*TV Times of the North* at that time). In 1968 she became production editor of *19*, then assistant editor, and finally editor.

She is single, lives in Covent Garden, loves travel, movies and is 'a complete believer in astrology'.

### *Patricia Lamburn*

Pioneer of a successful galaxy of women's and teenagers' magazines, director of IPC Magazines, Miss Patricia Lamburn was all but literally born into journalism.

Her mother, Nell Kennedy (Mrs F. J. Lamburn) was the originator of *Peg's Paper* —the magazine that became a household word. Her father, F. J. Lamburn, was the first editor of *Pearson's Weekly* and right-hand man of publisher-innovator Sir Arthur Pearson.

An inherited flair for anticipating readership needs, combined with accurate timing and a practical outlook, has notched up magazine after magazine to Patricia Lamburn's credit.

During the teenage boom of the sixties and early seventies, she became responsible for the editorial direction of *Honey* and *19*, *True, Look Now, Mirabelle*,

*Fabulous, Love Affair* and *Loving*. Publications reached peak circulations. 'It was all tremendously exhilarating.'

She began as a sub-editor on *Woman and Beauty* published by Amalgamated Press. After experience on the editorial staff of *Ladies' Home Journal* in America, she returned to England and magazine journalism here.

One of Patricia Lamburn's special interests has been the development of the popular real-life story magazine market. These publications satisfied the need for reassurance among women confused by a world 'in which traditional securities had been knocked sideways, and accepted standards were in total disarray'. Based on familiar, slightly larger-than-life situations with which women can identify, they present behavioural guidelines and characters who work out their own salvations, providing at the same time a vicarious emotional experience.

While making no magic claims for success, she feels that publications 'must reflect the feelings, attitudes and aspirations of their readers. If they try to impose attitudes they are bound to lose touch. Magazines need to keep pace with market changes and always to be flexible. And of course, the golden key to success is the right editor; one who can project his or her personality through the magazine so that it becomes a familiar friend to its readers.'

Not only fiction and features, but also advertising must reflect the readers' needs. 'We do not carry ads that are at odds with the magazines' contents, and we are very sensitive to their relationship with editorial. We would not wish to support the advertising of any product which could be deleterious to women, physically or psychologically.'

Her outlook for the future of women's magazines is optimistic. 'Successful magazines change all the time, constantly evolving and developing alongside their readers. Never before have there been so many opportunities for new publications. Women, today, are exposed to new concepts, ideas, environments, education and it is reasonable to suppose this trend can only accelerate.'


## Charlotte Lessing, *Editor of Good Housekeeping*

A circuitous path to journalism provided Charlotte Lessing with an unusually wide experience to bring to the editorship of *Good Housekeeping*. 'I started my working life at the age of seventeen looking after the classified advertisements on the *New Statesman*, she recalls.

Promotion to being 'the worst secretary Kingsley Martin [then editor] ever had' proved a dead-end. 'I moved on to the Royal Society of Medicine, and spent a year cataloguing medical films.'

Her break into journalism came as editorial assistant on the now defunct *Lilliput*, sister periodical to that other all-time classic *Picture Post*. No magazine could have demanded a higher standard or provided a more testing training ground. Her experience in everything from copy-tasting to subbing led ultimately to the post of cartoon editor.

During a nine-year absence to bring up her three children, she continued to freelance fiction and feature-writing.

Following a few years as public relations officer handling food and drink accounts, she was appointed twelve years back as deputy editor of *Good Housekeeping*. Three years ago she was appointed editor.

Her policy of providing features for an intelligent readership covering all aspects of life, and first-rate realistic, sensitively written fiction, ensures *Good Housekeeping*'s popularity with an exceptionally wide range of ages, from the young-married to the older woman.

### Deirdre McSharry, Editor of Cosmopolitan

A background in newspapers, travel, and some time in the theatre, plus humour and vitality, are what Deirdre McSharry brings to the challenging post of editor of the magazine for the liberated woman, *Cosmopolitan*.

Daughter of an Irish doctor with an East End practice who died when she was six, Deirdre, whose mother edited the Irish woman's magazine *Woman's Life*, read Celtic studies and English Lit. at Dublin University from the age of seventeen; and was orphaned when her mother, 'strong, hardworking, beautiful and funny, the strongest influence in my life', died three years later.

Leaving university for the theatre, Deirdre worked in late-night revue for the Gate Theatre Company, Lord Longford's company, and with Hilton Edwards and Michael MacLiammoir.

On tour in Egypt, Malta and Ireland, she wrote freelance pieces for Irish newspapers, working subsequently for the *Irish Times* and the *Irish Press*, before being appointed woman's page reporter for the *Evening Press*, Dublin.

Acceptance of some pieces in the *New York Herald Tribune* was followed by emigration to the U.S. and eighteen months with *Women's Wear Daily*, New York's daily fashion newspaper.

She travelled to Mexico via the Southern states, and then to London to become fashion writer for James Drawbell at *Woman's Own*. This was followed by the job of fashion editor on the *Evening News*, and women's editor for the *Daily Express*.

Three and a half years later she was fashion editor on the (then) sinking *Sun*, continuing when the paper was taken over by Rupert Murdoch.

Two years later she left *The Sun* with Joyce Hopkirk, woman's editor, when the latter started *Cosmopolitan*. 'After eighteen months, when Joyce returned to newspapers, I was made editor.'

Deirdre has three step-children, likes 'talking, reading, watching people, the theatre, dancing, cooking, country life at weekends, and being married.'

### Marjorie Proops

A stack of unanswered letters and a bowl of soup sparked off Marjorie Proops's career as Britain's best-loved advice columnist.

'I started this column by accident. I was woman editor of the *Daily Herald*. My advice columnist, Mary Marshall, died suddenly, leaving a legacy of unanswered letters.'

Unable to find a replacement, Marjorie took the letters home 'and sat up all night reading them, getting more and more distressed and distraught'.

Next morning she rang her friend, the psychologist Dr Eustace Chesser. He said, 'Bring a batch of these letters to my room at lunch time, and we'll have a bowl of soup and a chat.'

'There followed an extraordinary crash course, marriage guidance tuition, books to read, homework, until very nervously, and worried, I started to do the job myself. I can't pretend I had any burning desire to do this thing. It was something that had to be done. Gradually I found myself more and more concerned and involved.'

Soon after, Marjorie joined the *Daily Mirror* as a columnist, subsequently taking on a column in the *Sunday Mirror*. With the launching of the weekly *Woman's Mirror*, Marjorie's accurately described 'witty, pithy and wise' advice column became famous. Later her column gained an even wider public in the *Daily Mirror*.

Her entry into journalism began fortuitously. An ex-art student fashion-designer, teenage wife and mum, the war years saw her trudging her portfolio around the publishing houses. Discovering her talent for caption writing, fashion editor Julia Cairns asked if she wrote. Naively Marjorie replied that she wrote to her Service husband every day! 'Julia Cairns encouraged me to write monthly articles for the magazine *Good Taste*. This was the beginning of my journalistic career.'

Meeting Marjorie Proops, you are instantly impressed with her dignity, warmth, good humour and down-to-earth common sense that conceals an unusual depth of wisdom and understanding. The refreshingly frank, even disturbingly honest comments that came like a blast of fresh air after the soothing-syrup traditional to women's magazine advice columns, she attributes in part to her background. 'I grew up in pubs, and from a very early age learned to be gregarious.'

Two great influences on her life were her beloved, handsome, generous gambler father, and 'a Rabelaisian grandmother, a lusty woman who wore jewellery in bed, taught my sister and me to play poker, and sang us bawdy music hall songs instead of nursery rhymes.'

She became interested in Socialism early in her teens, and later in trade unionism.

'I've never been inhibited about sex, about the human body. I never moralise or wag fingers, nor make people's decisions for them. I am never shocked by what people do, only by their attitudes towards each other, by ignorance, intolerance and cruelty, the tribalism that exists in society.'

Assisted as she is by twelve highly trained staff, backed by a panel of experts, with an average of 35,000 to 50,000 problems a year from some thirteen million readers, Marjorie's job is no sinecure. 'I work twelve to fourteen hours a day, take some letters home at night, read and sign every reply, answer readers' telephone calls.'

She relaxes with 'unselective television viewing', bargello embroidery, bridge. Her chief pleasures are walking with, playing scrabble with, cooking for, and going supermarket shopping with 'Proopsy' her husband. 'I enjoy being a suburban housewife. I never wanted to be a smart Chelsea lady.'


*Jane Reed*

No one would doubt Jane Reed, editor of *Woman's Own* when she tells you that she began life with an ambition 'to do good for the world', for underlying a bubbling good humour, an enormously energetic, out-going personality, is an almost missionary zeal to serve her six million readers.

Initially, women's magazines did not attract her. 'I started out from business college thinking women's magazines were awfully ephemeral.'

A stint on *Modern Woman*, 'as a sort of cupboard turner-outer' converted her to the realisation 'that women's magazines were doing a tremendous amount of good, that they were a sort of fifth column of help and interest to women.' It is a fifth column infiltrating with beneficial results into more and more homes as circulations have taken an upward swing under her campaigning editorship.

'Women's power and influence have a far greater potential than they themselves yet realise.'

Under her imaginative sponsorship *Woman's Own* has not merely entertained; its surveys on marriage, women and work and other matters have benefited women in general. 'Lots of things we've campaigned for, the Government is now doing. The ordinary woman needs a voice, and we hope to embody that.'

In line with today's thinking she sees woman 'not as a mere mirror of her family, a wife and/or mother, but as an individual.'

While catering for the 'statistical woman' aged between twenty-five and thirty-five, married, with two children, a car, and a 'fridge', Jane Reed is acutely aware that no such thing as an 'average' woman exists, that 'attitudes are more important than age'. Also, that far from her owning a car or a 'fridge', there are many for whom a weekly women's magazine is their one 'luxury'. For this reason alone, she feels, 'they deserve something especially for themselves'. And that something, she is determined, whether helping them in the fields of law, finance, medicine, travel, cookery, fashion and furnishing or entertaining them with controversial features or fiction, shall be the best obtainable.

Following her debut at *Modern Woman*, Jane went to *Woman's Illustrated*, which folded, and then to *Honey*. She pays high tribute to *Honey*'s editor, Audrey Slaughter, 'I learned a tremendous lot from her.' Not without misgivings she gave up the assistant editorship of *Honey* to become fashion editor of *Woman's Own*, then was appointed editor some five years back.

She admits her initial mistakes with disarming honesty. 'I had a fixed idea of what the women of Britain wanted, and I did it for about two months. Those summer issues of 1970 *Woman's Own* would make your hair stand on end! They were totally unsuccessful. I went far too radical.'

Among the changes she initiated was a different type of cover. 'There were double heads, and all kinds of weird things, which resulted in dropped sales. It was very sobering for me to realise it wasn't successful.'

Her policies since have had happier results. She feels that *Woman's Own* is 'different' in 'catering for women who, while needing fundamental reassurance that what they are doing is right, also want a bit of a challenge. They don't want to feel they are being spoon-fed. I like to feel that *Woman's Own* is just a little bit more inquiring, a little more sensitive and aware of women's situation today than some of the other magazines.'

## *Josephine Sandilands, Editor of Woman*

Josephine Sandilands, recently appointed to the editorial chair of the giant popular weekly, *Woman*, began her career as a secretary in an advertising agency. She was about to start training as a copy writer when the chance of a career in journalism came up. This was on *King Magazine*, 'England's answer to Playboy', where for three years she 'did everything from writing the men's fashions to the astrology column' and learned the less glamorous, technical side of magazine publishing.

By way of contrast, 1965 saw her as women's editor of the bridal magazine *Woman, Bride and Home*. This was followed by the editorship of the magazine *Honey*.

Following her appointment as editor of *Duo*, a young home magazine which along with several others was aborted by the three-day week, she became associate editor of *Woman*.

She sees *Woman* as achieving a greater degree of realism to keep pace with women's changed and changing role in society, a bit more relevant to life today; as a journal which will help its readers to cope with current conditions and consumer problems, keeping slightly ahead of their needs, and also providing them with an enjoyable admixture of fiction which is slightly escapist, realistic and/or humorous.

Her hobbies are 'revitalising an old house; watching old movies; buying clothes, trying to keep her house plants alive'.

## *Lesley Saxby*

Exercising a behind-scenes judgment and discrimination that has proved invaluable to women's magazine fiction, is Miss Lesley Saxby, originator and editor of Macdonald and Jane's recently launched, highly successful Troubadour novels, and consultant fiction editor of *Woman's Own*.

A *Daily Telegraph* small ad started her career with publishers Cassell, Newman Flower, where her natural flair for recognising good fiction soon established her as a reader, first for this firm, and later as an 'outside' reader for publishers Hutchinson, Hurst and Blackett, W. H. Allen, and later, Granada.

Leaving Cassells she joined the editorial staff of the Hulton Press during the fabulous *Picture Post* era.

After a brief period as press officer for the Festival of Britain, she joined the women's magazine world as a fiction editor. Here her ability to project her own warmth and judgment proved a circulation-raiser for journals which included *Woman's Illustrated*, *Woman's Mirror*, *Petticoat*, and *Woman's Own*.

She feels that fiction, apart from merely entertaining, should also inform and, citing Dickens, and A. P. Herbert's 'Holy Deadlock' on divorce, even reform. She believes that history may often be better learned from fiction than from 'straight' reading.

Her recipe for fictional success is 'Good love stories about real people in real situations, but with a bit of depth, a bit of sparkle, and a bit of hope at the end.'

*Mrs Monica Tyson, Editor of Woman's Realm*

Mrs Monica Tyson, editor of *Woman's Realm* has a Diploma in Domestic Science that proved invaluable when she began her journalistic career as assistant editor of *Modern Woman* in 1958.

She has done freelance writing, which she enjoyed, and modelling which she 'simply hated'. She has appeared on television, and taken part in radio programmes ranging from news-items and phone-ins, to Woman's Hour and general interest programmes.

Her appointment as section editor of *Ideal Home*, was followed by four years as assistant editor, and nine years as editor.

She sees *Woman's Realm* as 'a service magazine catering for an older age group than *Woman*, or *Woman's Own*, but a younger one than *Woman's Weekly*'. Her typical reader 'would be about thirty-five, with growing children, probably living on a provincial suburban housing estate; intelligent, but without extended interest'. Equally she might be 'an older woman with grown-up children, needing reassurance and help in coping with today's changing values and current problems'. Fashion-wise, Mrs Tyson sees her readers as 'smart in a classical way, but not sexy, way-out or trendy'.

Mrs Tyson spends part of the week in London, but looks forward to her weekends at home with her family in Broadstairs, Kent.

# Bibliography

*A Booke of Good Manners*, Jacques Legrand, London 1487.

*A Booke of Strange Inventions called the First Parte of Needlework and a Schoolhouse of the Needle*, Jacques Legrand, London 1487.

*The Queen's Closet Opened*, London 1600.

*The Treasurie of Hidden Secrets*, London 1600.

*The Problems of Beautie and All Humane Affections* (translated by Samson Lennard from the Italian) by Tomaso Buoni, London 1606.

*The Table to the Compleat Cooke*, London 1639.

*The Ladies Cabinet Opened*, London 1639.

*The Queen's Cabinet Opened*, London 1655.

*The Ladies Garden*, London *c.* 1700.

*The Ladies Journal*, London 1727.

*The Ladies Magazine of the Compleat Library*, London 1738.

*The Ladies Magazine*, London 1770–96, and 1813.

*The Ladies Museum*, London 1781.

*The Lady's Pocket Magazine*, London 1790–96 and 1830.

*A Vindication of the Rights of Women* by Mary Wollstonecraft, 1792, ed. Miriam Kramnick, Pelican Books, 1975.

*La Belle Assemblée*, London 1796, 1818, 1826, 1831.

*Ladies Monthly Museum*, vols. 1–4, London 1807.

*Records of Weekly Amusements for the Fair Sex*, London 1815.

*National Magazine*, London 1833.

*The Toilet*, London 1843.

*Family Economist*, vols. 1–4, London 1848–55.

*Mayhew's London*, Spring Books, London 1851.

*The Englishwoman's Domestic Magazine*, ed. S. O. Beaton, vols. 6 and 8, London 1860–68.

*It Could Never have Happened* by Alice Head, Heinemann, London, 1939.

*Millions made my story* by Mary Grieve, Victor Gollancz, London, 1964.

*The Horizon Book of the Elizabethan World*, Hamlyn, London 1967.

*Victorian Advertisements* by Leonard de Vries and James Laver, John Murray, London 1968.

*The Edwardians* by J. B. Priestley, Heinemann, London 1970.

*Victoria's Heydey* by J. B. Priestley, Heinemann, London 1972.

*Dress, Health, Art and Reason* by Stella Newton, John Murray 1975.

*Dear Marje* by Marjorie Proops, Book Club Associates, London 1976. Modern women's magazines as listed in Chapter 9.

# Index

Universities, women's, 89

Vauxhall Gardens, 17
Victoria, Queen, 51, 68, 79, 94, *113, 126*
Victorian age, 51, *78, 80, 84, 86, 90, 95, 96, 135*
*Visiter, The,* 18
*Vogue,* 118, 119, 157

Walpole, Horace, 29
Ward, Joyce, 155
Warwick, Daisy, Countess of, 118
Wedgwood, Josiah, 21
Wellington, Duke of, 27, 45, 75
Wells, H. G., 109, 122, 167
Wesley, John, 77

Whistler, J. M., 74
Wilde, Oscar, 87, 89, 167
Wilkinson, Ellen, 147
William IV, King, 49
Wilson, Harriet, 27
Windsor, Duke of, 121
Winn, Godfrey, 149
Wolfe, General, 19
Wollstonecroft, Mary, 30, 76
*Woman,* 147, 167, 168, 169, 175, 176
*Woman and Beauty,* 171
*Woman and Home,* 142, 167
*Woman, Bride and Home,* 178
*Woman's Friend,* 142
*Woman's Journal,* 142, 165
*Woman's Life,* 172

*Woman's Mirror,* 155, *158,* 173, 176
*Woman's Pictorial,* 155
*Woman's Realm, 154,* 176
*Woman's Weekly,* 111, *143,* 157, 165, 176
*Woman's World,* 89, 91, 92, 101, 105
*Woman Worker,* 117, 157
*Women's Dreadnought,* 112
*Women's Illustrated,* 174, 176
*Women's Own,* 142, 167, 169, 175, 176
Workhouses, 51–2, *122*
Wren, Sir Christopher, 15

*Young Englishwoman,* 71, 76, 79, 81, 89, 90, 91, 92, *118*
Young, Francis Brett, 144

# ACKNOWLEDGMENTS

Grateful acknowledgment is made to the following for pictures reproduced in this book: Birmingham Reference Library, British Library, British Museum Newspaper Library, Colindale, Imperial War Museum, IPC, Leamington Spa Art Gallery, Leamington Spa Library, The Mansell Collection, The Mary Evans Collection, National Library of Ireland, National Magazine Company, Radio Times Hulton Picture Library, Spare Rib, Warwick Museum Services, Warwick Records Office.

For permission to use contemporary magazine covers for the jacket design of this book, the author and publisher wish to thank the publishers of *Cosmopolitan*, *Real Life Confessions*, *She*, *Spare Rib*, *Woman* and *Woman's Weekly*.